FEW ARE
CHOSEN

FEW ARE
CHOSEN

It's An Honor To Be
Selected By God

SAMETTE GEORGE

XULON PRESS

Xulon Press
555 Winderley Pl, Suite 225
Maitland, FL 32751
407.339.4217
www.xulonpress.com

Paperback ISBN-13: 978-1-66288-370-5
Hard Cover ISBN-13: 978-1-66289-157-1
eBook ISBN-13: 978-1-66288-371-2

Table of Contents

Introduction

Much of how we live our lives has to do with the choices we make. It may be something simple like where we will live or who we choose to live with. Our choices guide how we feel about our mate and our relationships. They determine how we raise our children and how we feel about their teachers and their school. It all has to do with our ability to make a choice. Our choices affect how we feel about our jobs, as well as others at our job. Our choices dictate how we feel about our neighbors and the neighborhood we live in. The way we feel about our parents and siblings all comes from making a choice; and, more importantly, how we feel or see ourselves. Many times, these decisions have to do with the information we receive before we make our mind up about how we are going to see or feel about something.

Choosing to see the glass halfway full, rather than halfway empty, plays a major role in everything that comes in front of us daily, especially when you must decide. It's not only things like where we live or how we feel about our mate or partner. It's not merely how we feel about our children, our job, neighbors, and family. The way we feel can go from one extreme to the next when we see that glass of water halfway empty, instead of halfway full. How you process information may have something to do with your beliefs. Something as simple as a weather report will read differently when you are a believer in the Word of God. When you're not a believer, forty degrees and sunny could be looked at as a really cold day and will have you thinking you'll have to stay in, because it's going to be too cold to go out. When you are a believer, all you will hear is the word sunny and you'll feel as though you don't want to miss the sunny day that God created, and you'll choose to go out while the sun is shining. The temperature being forty degrees won't play a major factor in your decision to go outside.

When my children, Samara and Aynyess, who are now ages twenty-nine and thirty, were young and still in elementary school, my husband, Curtis, and I would always say the same thing to them every day as they left the house to get on the school bus. We also said it well after they graduated high school. Even now as adults, I find myself saying it to them periodically, *"Have a good day and remember to make wise decisions."* We wanted them to believe that the choices they made could be good or could be bad. We also taught them that God does not give bad ideas; they only come from the devil.

I wrote this book to let others know that choosing God is the way they can live a more positive, healthy, and stress-free life. Try choosing to believe that there is something good in everybody and everything. No matter how grim the situation may be, if you choose to start looking for the silver lining in everything, you just might find it. Choose to believe in Christ as part of your daily routine. Believing in Him is like seeing the glass all the way full, every single day of your life.

Coming back from a short vacation with a cough and a little chest pain led me to believe I probably caught COVID, which forced me to go to the ER for testing, when I returned home. Within a matter of a few weeks, I was given a Stage 4 lung cancer and Stage 4 brain cancer diagnosis, along with a compromised spine diagnosis. I was told that it probably was not curable, but they would try to extend my days. The real details of that part of my journey come later in the book. But, I want you to know that it was because of my faith and strong belief in God that today I am a walking, talking, testifying miracle of the rewards of choosing to trust and believe in God. God does not make decisions for us, though, He gives us the gift of free will so that we can make decisions and choose to love Him. I pray that the story of my journey inspires you to want a closer walk with Him. And, for those who may not believe or are *on the fence*, my story will surely open your eyes to wanting that full glass, that only He can give.

> "If any man lacks wisdom, let him ask God,
> who gives generously to all without reproach,
> and it will be given to him."

> — James 1:5

Chapter 1

THEY SAID
*"Whose Report Will **You** Believe?"*

Throughout your lifetime, you will surely come across many challenges and disappointments that may be given to you in the form of verbal or written reports. It may be a denial for a bank loan that you've been hoping for and need so badly, and they said no. It could be that you applied to be accepted to the college of your dreams, and instead of getting a congratulations letter, you got a letter that started with "We regret to inform you," and found out it was a rejection of your college application. Maybe you worked hard at paying your bills on time and holding back on swiping your cards, but they said you still have a bad credit report that keeps you from getting that car you need so badly or that apartment. Maybe you found out that the perfect job for you, and the dynamics of your family, had been posted and you had all the qualifications to land it. Then, after updating your resume and applying, they said you were overqualified. I pray this hasn't happened, but possibly you've had a health issue that was a reason for concern, and you went to your doctor to have it checked out. He may have suggested that several tests be run before he would give a diagnosis, and maybe the reports came back positive for something you couldn't even begin to imagine would happen to you.

You must remember, God is always there in the midst of our storms, no matter how big or small, or how strong the winds blow. When you choose to invite Him into your heart, and trust and believe that all things are possible with Him, no matter what the reports may say, your storm that seemed out of control will be transformed into a beautiful spring shower. But, it starts with you not starting a pity party and inviting others to join you. My mom used to always say "misery loves company." Your friends may quickly accept your invitation and show up to bring you down more, instead of giving you words of encouragement. The information they have to contribute to the conversation may be exactly the kind of talk you don't need to hear. They may even tell you to invite God by praying, if you hadn't already done so. For the record, God does not attend pity parties; it's not His style. In the midst of a storm, you may pray for His help, but deep down, you don't really trust and believe. Instead, you've given up on the possibility that your situation will turn around. You get tired of waiting on God. You're impatient and believe it's too late. You start thinking that if it hasn't happened by now, it's not going to happen. To you, it simply seems like it's too big a problem, and you take the easy way out. Choose to speak life into those things that are positive and ignore those things that are negative. If you know what I know or have heard my story before, you will understand why I believe that God is the most powerful, positive force that we can choose to have in our life to guide and direct us in all matters.

I'm a witness that God does some of His best work in the midnight hour. Right when you think it's all over, He will show up and show out. The turnaround will be so unbelievable, you'll know it could *only* be God. That's right: that college rejection letter can and *will* be changed, when you truly humble yourselves and give the problem to Him to work out. The good credit report that you needed so badly to get that bank loan will mean nothing when God takes over. In case you haven't heard, He owns *all* the silver and gold. You believed the job you wanted so badly was no longer in sight, then you hear something happened to the candidate they had said was selected, and now the job is yours. The doctors told you the report says your illness is not curable and may have even given you time, like they said to me. But, God... He is the Great Physician and Jehovah Rapha. His report said, "By His stripes, you are Healed." His report said, "Heal me, Lord, and I will be Healed."

The attorney said, "The court report says it looks like you may have to serve some time." God is the Judge of all judges, and only He has the final word on your situation. God's report says, "Don't worry about anything, instead pray about everything." They said you weren't qualified, nor have had enough experience for the job. His report said, "Rest in the Lord: wait patiently for Him to act." The bank loan officer said that your credit score was too low, and you didn't have the collateral for him to approve the loan application. God's report said, "And it is He who will supply all your needs from his riches in glory, because of what Christ Jesus has done for us. Now tell me: Whose report will you believe?

Choose to have God in your *Journey of Life*, because from the time that you are born until the time that you die, you will be confronted with challenges, disappointments, bad new, good news, bad times, and good times. You'll have ups and downs, sad times, and glad times. When you travel this road of life, choose to receive the best help you can receive for everything, in all areas of your life. I did, and the blessings have been overflowing for me as far back as when I was a young child. God has showed up and showed out in my life in times when I believed there was no way the situation would end favorably for me. My life's journey with God by my side, when I didn't even know He was there, is one I want to share with others to help build up His kingdom. Remember, when they said "No," trust and believe that God said "Yes."

I was in my forties when I began to reflect on some of the personal experiences that had happened in my life since I was a young child, that made it crystal clear that there is a God in Heaven: A God who sits high and looks down low. Looking back and trying to recall how many times friends, family, teachers, banks, doctors, attorneys, and many others may have discouraged me from a dream, challenge, or belief simply by what they said, it was far from heartening. Many times, it was when things seemed hopeless for a particular situation, and instead of speaking words of encouragement and hope, they said the opposite. In some instances, other than my mom, they never said anything about having faith or believing that all things were possible with God. What they said never reflected *any* of God's reports, which made us want to give up and throw in the towel.

There is a time that comes when you no longer must wonder, but that you *know* you have been selected by God. You've had years of reading reports that never seemed to be in your favor: Years of dealing with situations that looked like there was no possible way they could change for your betterment. You dealt with years of tears and sleepless nights that seemed like they would never end. But, then you start wondering how it was that you overcame them all, when you realized there was no possible way. The problems were all too big, too impossible, too dark, time-after-time. All the reports said that the odds were against you. Then, you finally figured it out that you must have been chosen long before you ever realized there was such a thing. You started feeling honored, blessed, and highly-favored by God. You began to believe that just maybe, for reasons you don't understand, that yes, God chose me long before I knew of such a thing. Truly, He must have a purpose that is only for me. "Eye hath not seen, nor ear heard, and neither has entered the heart of man, the things God has prepared for those that love Him."

Many of the situations that are taken account of in my story, from age eleven until my sixties, I believe were all to prepare me for the most miraculous season in my life. From the beginning, the reports of my case and the diagnosis all pointed to a bad outcome for me. I'm sure that none of the bad reports throughout my life, including that one, were meant to purposely make me feel sad or discourage me from having hope. They said this, and they said that. They did not realize or remember there was another report. Whose report will you believe?

> "These things I have spoken unto you, that in me ye might have peace. In the world you will have tribulation. But be of good cheer; I have overcome the world."

> — John 16:33

Chapter 2

HE NEVER LEAVES YOU:
"Angels By Your Side"

When I was eleven years old, one day at school, I was at recess on the school playground, playing kickball. I fell on the macadam and scraped my knee badly. A teacher took me to the school nurse, who cleaned the wound and bandaged it, which allowed me to return to class. The nurse sent a note home with me for my mom, telling her I needed to have my knee looked at by a doctor. The next day, my mom kept me home from school and took me to the doctor. The doctor looked at my knee and re-dressed the wound. The doctor said he was getting ready to head out of town, but to be sure to go to the hospital emergency room in three days, and have the dressing changed one more time. I felt fine after leaving the doctor and was able to return to school the next day. My mom followed up three days later and took me to the hospital to have the dressing changed, like the doctor ordered. The nurse changed the dressing and instructed my mom to take the dressing off in another three days, and that it should be fine.

Three days later, while sitting in class, I began to shiver uncontrollably, and some of the kids in my class started laughing at me. The teacher saw what was happening and told me, "Stop it, right away."

Unfortunately, I could not stop myself from shaking and the other kids continued laughing, which made my teacher very upset. She said I was purposely disturbing the class and that she would have to send me to the principal for acting out. While sitting in the office waiting for the principal, the school nurse happened to walk through, and saw me sitting. She asked what I was doing there, and if I was in trouble. I explained what had happened in the classroom and that I was getting suspended for pretending to not be able to stop shaking. She immediately came over and put her hand on my forehead. She took me back to her office and took my temperature. The nurse told the principal that I was sick, and should not be suspended, but sent home for my mother to take me to see a doctor, because my temperature was 104 degrees. It was close to the school day ending, and because my mother did not drive and my father was at work in another town, they allowed me to stay and rest in the nurse's office, then just ride the school bus home. I was given a note from the school nurse to give to my mom, which said I should see a doctor right away. After my mother got home from work that evening, she read the note, and said she would take me to the doctor in the morning.

I don't remember much that evening after coming home from school, only that I felt tired and went right to bed. The next morning, I vaguely remember my mom helping me get dressed and getting in a cab. What I do remember is being in the emergency room and the nurse taking my temperature several times and saying, "Something is wrong with these thermometers." I remember the doctor coming in and my mom telling him I was delirious all throughout the night, and that as soon as it got light, she got me up and took me to the ER. The doctor checked my temperature, and agreed that the box of thermometers must be defective, and ordered the nurse to get a new box. After taking my temperature now for the fourth time, with the doctor present, they immediately took blood and checked me into the children's ward, but in a private, quarantined room. I remember that once I was taken to the room with my mom, she was told that I could not have any visitors, because gangrene had set into the knee, and I was very sick. I remember the doctor discussing with my mom that the infection in my knee had now begun to travel up my leg to my thigh. The doctor told my mom that if they did not get the infection under control, they would be looking at removing my leg to save my life.

It was a very lonely, sad time for me, being so young and not being able to see my mom, dad, or sisters. Back in 1969, there were no phones in the hospital rooms, and cell phones had not been invented yet. But, thank God, there was TV. It only had three channels, but at least it was some sort of entertainment. For several days, when I was quarantined, there was not much communication with anyone other than the nurses, who were in and out all day taking my temperature, giving me my medicine, checking my wound, and giving me my meals. I did have this one nice nurse in my room who sat by my side, monitoring me all day and night. She never really spoke to me, but she was there. I remember everyday, right after lunch, wanting to watch the "Dick Van Dike Show," but this other mean nurse would come in to get my empty meal tray, then turn off my TV, and tell me it was nap time. It made me so sad that I would even cry. But, like clockwork, the nice nurse would get up right after the mean nurse walked out of the room, and she would smile at me, then turn the TV back on so I could watch the "Dick Van Dike Show." It made me feel so good that she liked me and wanted me to be happy. I looked forward every day to watching the mean nurse collect my meal plate, turn off the TV, tell me it's nap time, and walk out of my room, only to watch the nice nurse turn the TV back on to Dick Van Dike.

As days went by, the antibiotics began to work on the gangrene infection and soon, I was feeling much better. After the fever broke, which was four days later, I was moved to another room, where there was another little girl. I now had a friend to talk to and they allowed my parents to visit. By the end of the week, the infection was under control, and I was feeling much better. The doctor met with my mother and said I could be discharged to go home and rest a few more days before going back to school. Because there were only a few days of school left before the school year ended for the summer break, my mom just kept me out and decided I did not need to go back that year.

Once I was home and feeling like my normal self, my mom asked me to share my visit at the hospital, since they did not allow her to spend much time with me there. I explained to her that I had a nice nurse who sat by my bed to keep me company, which was nice, and it kept me from feeling lonely. I also told her about the mean nurse who talked to me, but that it was always, "You need to eat all your food; you have to turn off the TV; you have to take a nap; you have to take this medicine; I have to give you this shot, etc." I told my mom how sad she made me feel and how she made me cry. I told my mom the only nurse that I liked and who made me feel good was the nice nurse, who would turn the TV back on every day after the mean nurse turned it off and told me it was time for me to take a nap.

My mom was big into sending "thank you" cards, and because she worked part time as a florist, they let her bring home the older flowers that they did not want to sell, because they would probably die in a few days or so. So, we always had flowers around our home. After sharing my story with her, she thought it would be nice to take the nice nurse a "thank you" card and flowers. So, we found a good card for her, and my mom made a small vase of flowers, and we headed back to the hospital to present the nice nurse with the gift.

After arriving at the hospital and going up to the children's floor, we went straight to the front desk nurse's station. My mom explained that I was a patient two weeks ago and that we were there to give my personal nurse a gift for treating me so nicely while I was away from my family, friends, and my home. My mom told her how we both were so happy and grateful that she treated me with so much love, when I *needed* to feel it in my time of need, and that the flowers and card were our way of saying "thank you" to the nurse for being so nice to me.

Unbelievably, the nurse at the desk was the head nurse and remembered me well. She said the flowers and card were a beautiful gesture, but unfortunately, they had been under-staffed for months, and that no one got a personal nurse who sat by their side, or that spent the whole day and night with one patient. She said they had too many sick children on that floor, and how she wished they could provide that type of ser-vice, but that they didn't. She also said I had *one* nurse, and described the mean nurse. She said that during most of my visit, when I was not being treated for the wound or given meals by the nurse she described, I was alone in my room. She said that in the beginning of my stay, I was delirious, but that was because of the high fever and that maybe I imagined this other nurse. To this day, I remember her well. She was all in white; she sat by my bed and kept me from feeling alone. I don't remember her speaking to me with a voice, but she would nod her head and always had a smile on her face, espe-cially when she would go behind the mean nurse after she left the room, and turn the TV back on to Dick Van Dike. The Word of God tells us, "He will never leave us, nor forsake us," and I'm a witness that that's the God's Truth of how He treats His children. I was too young at the time to truly understand who the unidentified nice nurse was, whom the hospital had no record of as my personal nurse while in quarantine, but as I have grown with life's trials, tribulations, and challenges, I'm certain she was an angel that God sent to watch over me and guard me during my hospital stay.

> "For He will command his angels concerning you to guard you in all your ways. On their hands they will bear you up, lest you strike your foot against a stone."

> — Psalm 91: 11-12

Chapter 3

HE MAKES A WAY:
"Nothing is Too Big or Small for God"

I n my early twenties, I was blessed to be able to open my first beauty salon, because of what God had laid before me at an early age. I had a close family member who was working in the cosmetology industry as a hair stylist at his aunt's salon. My cousin, Rodman, had a slip-and-fall accident and broke his arm. He was still able to do hair, but was instructed by his doctor not to let the cast get wet. I was only fourteen, and had just started Vo-Tech at our local high school. He knew that I was in cosmetology class and asked me if I could come to the salon after school for a couple of months and shampoo for him, while his arm healed, so he could continue to service his clients. I asked my mom and she thought that because it was only a few blocks away from the school, it would be a great opportunity to get some real-world experience and my foot in the door of a nice, recognized salon. I took the job that he offered me while he had his cast on, and I ended up staying with him for four years, until after graduation. During that time, I fell in love (so I thought) and got married weeks after graduation, to only end up back at my parents' home eight months later and working back at Rodman's salon. After six months of being back, I fell in love again, remarried, and followed my new husband out of state where he was working, and once again, after one year, found myself back at my parents', finalizing a divorce, and working back at Rodman's salon. After about another year of working with him and closely watching the day-to-day operations of how the salon was managed, I felt confident enough that I thought the next move for me would be to open my own salon. Rodman gave me his blessings and allowed me to continue working at his salon, until the doors to my salon were ready to open.

I opened the salon as planned, as well as a sister salon on the other side of town, and I ran them both smoothly and successfully for three years. At the end of the third year, I decided to close the two smaller salons, and combine the two at another location to have one large salon. It was running around, rather than trying to manage the operations and employees at two different locations. Everything was beautiful with the salon, the employees, and the clients. I was making money and felt successful as a salon owner at the young age of thirty. But, when it seemed like everything was perfect, I received a letter from the IRS, requesting a meeting with them regarding taxes. Unfortunately, I was so busy making money and building up employees, clients, and the integrity of the salon, that I neglected to pay taxes that were due on the business, and withheld from the employees' paychecks. I knew the meeting was going to be bad, but had no idea how bad it was for me and the business.

At the meeting, they explained that because I neglected to pay the government their share of what was owed and that I had not made arrangements to make payments and catch up, they would be attaching my assets for payments. I was told that in five days, they would send a representative to my business to sit at the reception desk, and that for every ten dollars I collected for services to clients, they would take eight dollars. They were also going to attach a sticker to certain valuable salon equipment that would say, "This property cannot be sold or moved from the location by order of the IRS." They were also going to put a levy on the property I was buying that was ordered by the court, and that maybe it could not be refinanced or sold until the IRS received their balance, which was thirty-six thousand dollars. It was a beautiful fifteen-room duplex that housed the salon on the first floor, and my living quarters on the second and third floor. I was told that the worst-case scenario was that they had the authority to shut the business down. At the same time, the man who I bought the house from sold me the house on a sales agreement, and gave me five years to get conventional financing from a bank, and the five years was now up. He made it clear that he would not extend the agreement and that if I did not have the financing in place by the end of the month, we would have to move out. It was one of the most stressful times of my life. I was so worried about my employees, who had homes and families that depended on their income to survive. I was so embarrassed and did not know what to do, but cry and pray for God to work it out.

A friend advised me that I should file bankruptcy to keep the IRS from setting up shop at my business, as well as stop the levy against my property. Time was running out and I knew I had to do something, so I looked in the phone book and contacted a bankruptcy attorney, in the hopes that she could help me. I read the notice from the IRS to her over the phone. She explained that she could put a stop to it, but that there was not much time. I would need to meet her at her office at 6:00 a.m. the next morning and bring her $5000.00. She said she could prepare the documents and be in bankruptcy court by 8:00 a.m. to file. So, I wrote her a check for the $5000.00, which was almost all the money I had in the world, and was at her office by 6:00 a.m. She explained she would be filing a "Chapter 11" bankruptcy, which would eliminate my credit card balances and current utility bills. The bankruptcy would divide my debt with the IRS over a period of five years, and would halt the levy they would place on my property. It would also stop those annoying calls and notices from the IRS or other creditors. She said payments would not start for sixty days, which gave me a breather and allowed me to save up a little money. With tears in my eyes, I thanked God over and over again for removing that IRS burden. But, I was not out of the woods yet. I still had to get the property financed before the end of the month or I would have to close the salon and find somewhere to live. It was a scary time in my life. I continued to pray every day that God would continue to help me out of this mess.

The Bible tells us that faith without works is dead. So, I pulled myself together and began to work on getting the financing. I went to my bank where my business and personal accounts were kept, as well as the man's mortgage who had sold us the property on a sales agreement. I met with the loan officer, and they told me that there was nothing they could do, and that they no longer were offering assumable mortgages on notes at their bank. I continued to pray, knowing that I would not give up. I went to another bank, where my friend Mamie's husband was a loan officer. She had put in a good word with her husband and set up an appointment a few days later at 8:00 a.m. for me to meet with him. I was feeling good about the upcoming meeting and began to prepare for it right away. I gathered some documents and put together some talking points to help sell myself and my desperate need to have my house financed. The morning of the meeting, I got up extra early, put on a nice business suit and made sure my hair and makeup looked nice. I got in my Corvette and drove downtown to the bank, not realizing how busy downtown was in the morning. There were many state office buildings downtown and many state workers all looking for parking spaces, and trying to get to their jobs by 8:00 a.m. After finding myself downtown riding around for more than thirty minutes, looking for a parking space and noticing it was getting closer and closer to 8:00 a.m., I began to panic.

I knew that my friend, Mamie, had set up a special appointment and that the appointment was so early because her husband was squeezing me into his schedule as a favor. I knew that if I did not make it, there was no telling when he would be able to get another time to help me. As I drove around, I had been listening to gospel music and feeling good, but once I realized that I would probably miss my appointment, I began to cry. The more I thought about missing out on someone who could help me, the crying got more intense. It was to the point where the crying was uncontrollable, and I truly felt like I was losing it. As I continued to drive around, I finally saw an empty parking space, but as I went for it, I was cut off and another driver quickly pulled into the space where I was going to park. At that point, the crying seemed to have gotten louder and I felt like I was having a nervous breakdown. Right at that moment, when I was listening to the Clark Sisters singing "I'm Looking for a Miracle," out of nowhere, it no longer sounded like the three sisters singing, but behind me in my two-seater Corvette, I could hear a whole choir of angels singing. It seemed as if the car was driving itself, and was not even on the macadam. The car actually began rocking back and forth, while the choir got louder and louder. Then, all of a sudden, I felt the warmest embrace from my head to my toes, like someone was holding me. At this point, I was sure I was losing my mind, but when I looked up, I was right in front of the bank, and there was an open parking space that I was able to pull into at 7:58 a.m. I thought, *wow*! Was what I had just gone through all in my imagination? It had to be. But, before I got out of the car, I `looked into the rear-view mirror to check myself, and my hair was all over the place, and my face was covered with running black mascara, as if I had been through a wild ride. I quickly cleaned myself up and ran into the bank.

After meeting with the loan officer, he said he could only approve the loan if I paid off a large credit card bill at John Wanamaker's, and came up with $15,000.00. He was able to put it in writing and told me to get back with him as soon as possible. It was not the response I wanted to hear, but it was someone who was willing to work with me. I went home and prayed on how this could work for me. I did not have the $15,000.00 or the $2,700.00 to pay off the credit card. I continued to pray to God for His help. That evening, something told me to go back to my bank and let them know that another bank was willing to help me, but with a few stipulations. Once I explained what the stipulation from Mamie's husband's bank was and showed them the letter in writing from the other bank, out of nowhere, the loan officer at my bank said they would not only match it, but that since my mother was a good customer and my business was doing well, that they had a better offer. They said that I would have to meet the same stipulations, except for the $15,000. They said I would only need $10,000.00, but they were sure they could do it and wanted to keep my business at their bank. Time was running out with the man who sold me the house, but I felt like something was happening, and thanked God.

Honestly, the next two weeks were so unbelievable for me. I remember calling John Wanamaker to double check my balance, so that I knew exactly what I needed to pay them off, which was one of the stipulations to getting the mortgage approval. I knew it was a little more than $2,300.00, because I had bought an expensive fur coat a few weeks back. When the representative came back to the phone after checking the computer, she told me that my balance was only $295.00, and I could not believe it. I remember asking her if I came out that evening and paid the $295.00, could she give me a print off that said I had a zero balance with them? She said, "Yes, but we are closing in thirty-five minutes."

I quickly got into my car and drove as fast as I could to the mall, paid them the $295.00, and sure enough, got a printout that said I had a zero balance with their store. So, that was one stipulation already met. Wow! What a thank you prayer to God I remember saying that night.

A few days later, my sister, Marsha, was listening to the radio, and the day they spun the birthday wheel, it landed on November 24th. She knew it was my birthday. The station was looking for the first caller who had that birthday. She quickly called in and used my name. At the time, all they needed was my actual birthday with the year, my phone number and address, to win the prize. It was great because she knew them all from memory. They said when she came to redeem the prize at the station, that they would need to see a driver's license. When I went to the station to redeem the prize, it was $1000.00. I could not believe it. So, now all I needed was $9000.00.

A few days later, I went into my closet to put on a pair of boots that I had not worn in a year or more, and when I went to put my foot in, the toe was stuffed with something. When my hand felt inside the boot and pulled out the stuffing, it was $5000.00 that I recalled myself hiding years before from a court settlement I had received. I knew I had hidden money in my boot years before, but thought I had used it all. All I could say was, "Thank you, Jesus!" Now, I only needed $4000.00. During that time, God sent me a new boyfriend named Curtis, who I later realized was a helpmate sent from God. He was excellent in the buying, trading, and selling game. He told me to sell a few things to get extra money, and I did. Because I did not have to pay any bills for sixty days from filing the bankruptcy, I was able to hold on to my money. We ended up having a good, profitable two weeks at the salon, and by the end of the month, I had come up with the entire $10,000.00. A few weeks later, I did get a call from Wanamaker's telling me that there was a glitch in the computer the evening I came in, and that my real balance was about $2000.00, not $295.00. At that point, I didn't care, because by then, the mortgage had already been processed and finalized. The glitch served its purpose for getting me the zero balance print off when I needed it. I knew then that God could touch anyone or anything, including computers.

> "I will lead the blind by ways that they have not known, along unfamiliar paths I will guide them; I will turn the darkness into light before them and make rough places

smooth. These are the things I will do; I will not forsake them."

— Isaiah 42:16

Chapter 4

Only God Gives Life:
"For This Child, We Prayed"

As time went by, things straightened out with my salon and I was in a good place. Much of how I was feeling was because my helpmate, who I prayed to God to send me, turned out to be so much more. It turned out that he soon became my best friend. After one-and-a-half years of dating, he proposed, and we were married in Jamaica at the couples' resort called Sandals. They had only been open one year and my sister, Marsha, who won me the extra cash I needed from the radio birthday wheel, also won an all-expense paid trip to Sandals. While she and her husband were in Jamaica, Curtis proposed to me, and I said yes. When she returned, I told her the good news that we were getting married. Immediately, she said, "You got to go to this place called Sandals; there were couples getting married at the resort and it was beautiful."

So, we took her advice and started planning a wedding at Sandals in Jamaica. A few months later, we took a small group of thirteen friends and family members, and were married on the beach at sunset. We could not have been happier.

Together, we turned the property that God was able to save from the IRS and from the man who sold it to me on the five-year sales agreement into more than a house where I had my salon and lived, it was now a home. It was a wonderful time.

During the first two years of marriage, we put a lot of work and money into our house. We re-landscaped the outside and added a deck, fencing, and an inground pool. We planted beautiful flowers and purchased new outdoor furniture. Our home was right on the corner of a main street, and truly was a showplace. We continued the inside with renovations that separated our living area from the salon area. It gave us more privacy, and it allowed us to come and go from our home, without crossing the salon space. Life was good, but I kept feeling like something was missing. I was not sure what it was until I found myself crying when I saw a family in the playground with their children. If I saw a woman with a baby or a mound below her breast, I would cry. I really did not understand why this was happening to me. Then, it hit me one night when I was watching a movie called *What to Expect When You're Expecting*. By the end of the movie, I was a mess, and Curtis wasn't sure why I was so upset, especially because it wasn't a tearjerker movie. It was then that it hit me: I wanted to have a baby. I told Curtis and explained that what was missing from our beautiful home was children. We discussed it all night, and together we concluded that we should start a family. I was already thirty-five years old and did not know that it would be more difficult. After two months of trying, and no pregnancy, we decided to make an appointment with my OB-GYN and see if they could help.

After meeting with the doctor, having several tests run, and fertility work to make sure we were both equipped properly with what we needed for me to conceive, the doctor said we were both good and should not have any problems. She said that my eggs were older and much smaller than the eggs of a twenty-year-old, which could make it a little harder for Curtis's sperm to find a target. She suggested taking a round of Clomid, which is a fertility drug used to plump eggs up, so they would be an easier target for Curtis's sperm. We took her advice. We were amazed and blessed that after one round of taking the drug for three days, by the end of the week, I was pregnant, and we thanked God.

Four weeks later, I went and had an ultrasound that the doctor scheduled me to take at a different office. During the ultrasound procedure, I began to suspect something was wrong. When the technician called in another technician to look at the monitor, then sent for a doctor to look at the monitor. It was soon after the doctor took a look, that he informed me there was no heartbeat, and I had what was called a blighted ovum. He explained that what happened was that soon after conception, the embryo stopped developing and left the sac empty, with an expired egg. It was one of the saddest days of my life. He told me that I would need to come back the following week to have a D & C procedure to have the material in my uterus removed. He told me it was not healthy to carry around a dead fetus, and that it had to be done. I left the doctor's office hysterically crying. As soon as I arrived home, I went straight to our garage, where Curtis was working on his motorcycle. He saw me crying and reached out to comfort me. He knew I had been to the doctor to have an ultrasound of the baby, which led him to believe something was wrong without me having to say anything. After I explained the blighted ovum, we cried together. We wanted a baby more than anything, and the thought of us losing our baby was devastating.

A few days later was Sunday, and we went to church as always. When the pastor asked to please stand up if there were any testimonies from this week, I nudged Curtis that I was about to stand up. I decided to share what the doctors had told me about the blighted ovum, because we had recently announced to our church family that we were expecting a baby. I asked the church to pray for us, because we were having a difficult time accepting the report from the doctor. The pastor called me up to the front of the church, along with the elders of the church, and they laid hands on me, and prayed that God would comfort our minds and bless us with a baby. Many of the church members told us that they would be praying for us as well. The next week, when I went back to the doctor for the D & C procedure, I remember lying on the table while the technician performed another ultrasound. I laid there with tears in my eyes, as I prepared my mind for the cleaning out of my uterus.

The technician noticed that I was crying and asked me what was wrong. I told her I really wanted a baby, and now my baby was gone. She said she did not understand. While crying, I explained that on my last visit they were not able to find the baby's heartbeat, and that I had been diagnosed with having a blighted ovum. She looked at me and said, "Stop crying, here's the baby's heartbeat." She pointed to the monitor that was connected to a wand and showed me a small blinking light on the baby's ultrasound. I thought I was dreaming. I lifted my head from the table and said, "Did you say that's a heartbeat?"

Her answer was, "Yes!"

I could not believe it. Everything was okay. We had a baby with a heartbeat. They gave us the due date, and eight months later, we delivered a beautiful baby girl named Samara. We did run into a serious complication minutes before I delivered my daughter. It was called "abruption of the placenta." It got kind of scary for me. Ten minutes after we got into bed for the night, my belly started getting tighter and tighter, until it was beginning to get uncomfortable, when suddenly, I heard a pop sound that came from my belly, followed by a gush of water, or what I thought was my water that had broken. I called my doctor to let him know that my water had broken, but that I didn't have any real contractions and was prepared to stay home as long as possible, or if I could endure the labor pains, without needing medication. He said that would be okay. He asked me to describe the water, with questions like, "Does it look clear? And is it gushing out or dripping out?"

I told him that the water wasn't clear, that it was reddish, and that the water was gushing out every time I moved. He told me to come into the hospital for a check-up, and then I could go back home and try to relax as long as I could. I didn't know how serious the situation was that I was going through and took my time, adding a few more baby items to my prepacked hospital bag. When my husband saw that I was shaking out of control, he made me stop doing what I was doing, and got me to the car right away. We headed straight to the hospital that was only three miles from our home.

When we pulled up to the ER, I saw where there were attendants with a gurney out in the driveway. I told Curtis that there must have been a bad accident, and that they were probably waiting on the ambulance and instructed him to go around and park in the parking lot. As we were walking toward the entrance of the ER, one of the attendants looked down at my legs, and could see the reddish fluid dripping down. He immediately said, "Are you Mrs. George?"

I answered yes.

He said, "We've been waiting on you," and before I knew it, they quickly lifted me onto the gurney and took me straight to the operating room.

When we got there, my doctor yelled, "Where have you been? I been here for thirty minutes, and I live twenty miles from here." He was furious and said there was no time to explain. They quickly undressed me, while they were helping Curtis get dressed for the operating room.

They quickly put an IV in my arm, covered my mouth and nose with a plastic mask and that's all I remember, until I woke up from surgery.

Once I was wide awake and settled in my room, along with Curtis, the doctor came in to speak with us. He immediately said that the baby seemed to be fine, but was having a little trouble breathing, so she was put in the NIC-U to be watched closely for the next few days. He went on to explain that I experienced what was known as an abruption of the placenta, which is very serious. It's when the placenta pulls away from the uterus and you begin to hemorrhage. The mother loses a lot of blood, and the baby is literally drowning in blood. There is a fifty-fifty chance that the mother or baby can die. He told me that she was okay for now, but that I needed a blood transfusion ASAP, and that if I even tried to get out of bed, that my blood level was so low I would probably pass out. So, I got the blood transfusion. Samara was released from the NIC-U after three days, and was breathing on her own, with no problem. It was scary, but once again, God helped me, and the baby passed the unfavorable reports. Thank you, God.

> "See now that I, I am He, and there is no God beside Me; It is I who put to death and I who give life. I have wounded, and it is I who heal, and there is no one who can deliver from the power of My hand."

> — Deuteronomy 32:39.

Chapter 5

A House is Not a Home: "As For Me and My House, We Will Serve the Lord"

A few years later, after the birth of our second child, Aynyess, Curtis and I started thinking a lot about their future education. We wanted to make sure they would be prepared for college and a successful future. The school district that we lived in had begun having problems with their budget, the teachers, and students. It appeared their ranking had dropped and there were lots of rumors surfacing that many of their graduates were not doing well on the PSSA testing (Pennsylvania System of School Assessment). That information, to us, was a red light that maybe we should investigate private schooling or look for a new school district. We loved the house that we made into a home, but started thinking that maybe our home needed to be moved to an area or school district that would be more conducive to our girls getting the best education available.

For more than two years, we looked here, there, and everywhere, trying to find a nice home for our family. It seemed like the search was never going to come to an end, and mainly because we were specific about what we needed. We had told the agent years before that we would need a ranch-style house, with a living room, family room, and a recreation room. And, that it was important that it had at least three bathrooms, a large kitchen, and dining room. The home had to have space for me to have a small in-home salon, in-law quarters, an in-ground swimming pool, and a big backyard for my girls and family barbeques. These requests were all deal breakers in selecting a house, and the agent was still aware of our needs. After looking at fourteen houses, we were contacted by our real estate agent, and he urged us to take a second look at a house we looked at more than a year ago. When we initially went to look at the property, I looked at the broken fence, the sheet or blanket in the window, and the unkept landscaping that turned me off to the point where I did not even want to go inside to see more. What the agent did tell us was that the listing price had dropped more than $90,000.00, along with a decrease in the property taxes from a new property reassessment. He said that the outside didn't get any better and that there was a lot more wrong on the inside, but that he knew Curtis was a *Jack of All Trades.* He believed that for the price, with work that Curtis could do, we could really come up on the property. The second owner had gotten divorced seven years prior, and after his wife left, he let the house go, and anything in the house that could be broken *was* broken.

I discussed it and decided to take a second look. So, we contacted the agent and booked for it to be shown to us again.

I attempted to put myself in a positive mindset and forget about our initial encounter at the property. When we pulled up, I saw where the agent was not lying; it looked the same or *worse* on the outside. But, based on all the other homes on that block, I knew it was a nice neighborhood. The neighborhood was one of the nicest in town, and all the homeowners were professionals. On that block, ninety percent were doctors and attorneys. It was one of the wealthiest neighborhoods in our town and the homes, in my opinion, were absolutely beautiful. In fact, the agent told us that the home we were looking at was built by the first CEO of the Giant grocery store chain. As we were entering the house, I felt something, something *good*. Without even looking at the entire place, I could about see most of it from the foyer, because of the open floor plan. I remember standing on the foyer platform and pointing, while saying the name to different rooms. I saw the living room, dining room, family room, rec room, and swimming pool, then said, "I think this is our house," even though the living room ceiling was on the floor from a bad leak. I felt something, quickly went through the house, and found a small room where I could put a salon, as well as a fully-finished lower level that would serve perfectly for our mom. The house had an extra bedroom and bathroom. I prayed for this house, and God lead me to it. It was a fixer-upper, and I recalled that I did not ask God to send me a house that didn't need any work; this one did have everything I prayed for in a house. By the time the agent finished showing the property, we made an offer, and a few days later, we received a call that the seller had accepted, and was giving us ninety days to secure financing and to go to settlement. I knew from the time we walked in, that it was my dream house, and I had to have it. Curtis agreed.

Immediately, we started looking for financing and put our house up for sale. We would need the proceeds from the sale of our house to use for the balance down payment. We had a hard time finding a bank to give us a mortgage, and had to turn to a mortgage broker for help. Their interest rates were much higher, plus they had fees they charge for finding the funding for your project. We were able to get a commitment from a broker, who assured us that, based on the information we gave on the application and receiving certain documents that they requested us to submit, they would be sending out an approval letter, as well as a settlement date. We were feeling better than blessed and started preparing for the move. We rented a moving truck and arranged for help on moving day. I started checking out childcare for my three-year-old, and registered my five-year-old into kindergarten in the school district, where we would be moving. I made a flyer and hung it in my salon. It informed the clients that after thirteen years in business, and twenty-four years of doing hair, that I would be retiring to be a stay-at-home mom. I assisted my staff with relocating to other salons, or, in one case, a stylist was able to open her own salon. We were packing a little every day and things could not have been better. At least once a week, from the time the seller accepted our offer, we would drive to the new neighborhood, just to drive by and glance at the house.

It was one week away from settlement day, with plans to move the following day. Everything was ready to go. We confirmed our plans, and boxes were packed and waiting to be put onto the moving truck. The Thursday before the scheduled Monday settlement, we took a ride to the new neighborhood to glance at our house, and we saw the seller out at his mailbox. We stopped to say hello and to let him know that we were excited about the settlement on Monday. Somehow, we got into a conversation with him about moving, and we told him that our scheduled moving date was planned for the day after the settlement. He was impressed that we were all packed up and ready to move out immediately. I told him we did not want to waste any time, and since he had already moved out, it was possible for us to come to the house on Saturday and do some cleaning. He said it had already been cleaned, but that if we still wanted to come and put our finishing touches on the place, that would be fine. He told us that we could not move any of our furniture in until after the settlement was final, then gave us the keys for us to come on Saturday.

I immediately called my sisters, Marsha and Stevie, who told us they would help, and we let them know that on Saturday we would be cleaning and asked if we could count on them. They both said that they had previously made plans for Saturday, but were both available on Friday after work. Since that was their only time to help before the settlement on Monday, I said okay to Friday, and thought that it probably didn't make a difference since the house was already vacant and we had the keys. So, we got together early Friday evening and cleaned until 10:00 p.m. I was glad that we did not listen to the seller when he said the house had been cleaned, because it was not up to my expectations. When we saw how nice and clean the house was after my sisters and I did our thing, I came up with the idea that since we had a clean house and an unplanned Saturday, that we should at least take our boxes over and hang our art on the walls. Before we knew it, noon had come, and the boxes were in their assigned rooms, and the art looked fabulous on the walls. Why I had the crazy idea to spend the rest of the day moving the things we could move onto Curtis's truck, with the help of his friend, Stew, into the house, I do not know. But, we did start the move without the permission of the seller. When we looked at our current home Saturday night and saw that it was practically empty, we thought that we might as well take Sunday and complete the move, which we did, and moved in. We figured that the next day, we would be moving in after the 10:00 a.m. settlement anyway, and we already had been given the keys. Our first night in our new home looked beautiful, and felt so good. We loved it and it felt like we were on vacation. We forgot that we had invited our good friends, Pam and Mason, from Maryland to come visit us on Sunday, when we thought we would still be in the old house. So, we called them and explained that things had been expedited with our move, and told them to still come, but to the new address. We had a great afternoon with them in our new house. It appeared that things had been simplified, so we thought.

Monday morning, we were up bright and early for settlement day. The girls stayed at my mom's house for the weekend, so they would not get in our way during the cleaning party with my sisters, which was perfect because their last day at daycare was on Friday, and the start of the new daycare and school wasn't for another two months. We arrived at the attorney's office about 9:45 a.m., and were stopped and greeted at the entrance, which I thought was a little strange. The receptionist told us that Lee wanted to meet with us in his office, not in the settlement suite. When we went in and sat down, he immediately told me there was a problem. He said that the seller was in the settlement suite, and was not a happy camper. He further went on to tell us that when the lender did the final credit check that morning, a tax bill came up from a prior relationship of mine years before, as never being paid. Lee told us that funding the mortgage had been put on hold by the broker until we could show that it had been paid. He said it was best if we did not go to the settlement suite and meet with the seller. He suggested that we leave and contact the broker ASAP, while he pacified the seller, and tried to put him on hold for a few days. I was devastated, and all I could do was cry.

We went directly home and called the broker. He answered his phone right away and apologized for having to cancel the settlement, but that it was out of his hands. He said he was sorry that it looked like things were going wrong, but that he was working on making it right. He asked me to please try to stop crying and worrying, and to give him a day or two to work on it. In the meantime, the seller came back to the house after he left the attorney's office. When he saw that we had taken the liberty to move in without first completing the settlement, he was furious, and reminded us that he told us that we were not to move any furniture into the house, and that we said we were just cleaning. He reminded us that he was an attorney and he had heard stories about how squatters move into one's house, and how hard it was to get them out.

We assured him that we were not squatters, and that our broker was working on getting things straightened out, and to please give us a few days. He said, "Absolutely not," and that we had to be out by 6:00 p.m. the next day, or he would call the police. Curtis had been back and forth with calls to the broker all evening, but I was too upset, and could not even speak with him. All I did all night was pray and cry, pray and cry. I called my mom early the next morning to see if she could hold onto the girls for another day and night, because we may be moving back into the old house that we just moved out of. I explained to her what had transpired in the last twenty-four hours and how bad the situation had gotten.

After she heard the details of the mess that I made by sneaking in early, she suggested that I go up to our church at 10:00 a.m., and ask the Tuesday prayer group to pray with me. My mom was one of the most powerful prayer warriors I knew, so when she said to go, I went. After hearing my situation, they agreed that we needed some powerful praying.

They prayed with me for an hour and encouraged me to keep the faith, trust, and believe that God would see us through. It made me feel good, and gave me the confidence I needed at that time. Once I got back in my car and checked my phone, I saw where Curtis had called me four times, so I immediately returned his call. When he answered, he asked where I was. I reminded him that I had gone up to the church to meet the prayer group. He told me that we had fifteen minutes to get back to the attorney's office, so to come home right away and pick him up. He said that the broker called an hour ago and said he had worked it out, and had notified the attorney that we had the green light to settle. He said they already had notified the seller and they were all at the settlement table, waiting on us. I was so happy, that I was shaking. Not only were our prayers answered, but answered quicker than we could imagine. I picked Curtis up, and we rushed to get to the settlement. We were about ten minutes late, but we made it there. Everyone was waiting for us at the settlement table. We apologized for being late and quickly moved through the documents that needed to be signed. They gave us the completed paperwork and handed us another set of keys. We thanked everyone, and we were out. I cried the entire way back to our new home, but this time, they were tears of joy. The house was now our home, and only remained our home because of God's love. Truly, we serve an awesome God.

"It shall also come to pass that before they call, I will answer; and while they are still speaking, I will hear."

— Isaiah 65:24

Chapter 6

A Rainbow for Us:
"Our Sign for Protection,
Hope and Life"

A few months after moving to our new home and getting the girls started with daycare and school, I realized that the *stay-at-home* mom dream didn't pay much. In fact, it didn't pay anything. It felt good and I got a lot of love back from Curtis and the kids, but no cash. We had arranged for one of the rooms to be a salon suite so I could make a few dollars, but because of the zoning in our neighborhood, it wasn't legal, and I had to sneak clients in and out of the house for salon services. Because of the hassle, I only took appointments on Wednesdays and early Saturday morning. Because of my limited schedule, I found myself in a large, beautiful, prayed-for house most days alone, and began to get bored. My best friend, Sis, suggested that since I had my cosmetology teacher's license, that I consider substitute teaching at our local Vo-Tech, that was only minutes away from our home. I checked it out and it sounded perfect. I did not have to make a commitment until the morning that they requested me to cover for a teacher who was absent, and I could be home from work before the girls came home from daycare and school. I took my friend's advice and signed up. I was a substitute at the Vo-Tech for about two years. When the cosmetology program director was close to retirement, my friend, Sis, the principal, asked me to apply for the position. I hadn't thought about a commitment like that, but was spending three or four days at the school already. So, I applied and was offered the opportunity to be the Director of the Cosmetology program full-time. After talking it over with Curtis, we both looked at that opportunity as a blessing.

I took the job assignment and loved it. They gave me free reign to write my own curriculum, and to redesign an antiquated program. The students thought it was great and quickly adapted to my style of teaching. By the end of my first year, the program had a waiting list of more than fifty students who wanted to enroll in the cosmetology program. I took every professional development class that I could to keep up with the trends in the cosmetology industry, as well as new teaching styles to help retain students. Not to pat myself on the back, but I was looked at by the students, parents, peers, administrators, and the superintendent, as one of the top teachers in the school district, and had the awards and accolades as proof. I was the bomb teacher, and loved every minute of it! Truly, it was my dream job. It was a chance for me to not only show off my skills, but to share them with a young group of upcoming stylists. I loved telling the students stories about my personal experiences as a practitioner. For me, it was the best.

After teaching for nine years, I convinced Curtis to start substitute teaching at the Vo-Tech school. He was a certified building trades instructor, and loved working with young people, like me. He signed up and started subbing right away. They moved him between building trades and some of the other traditionally male shop classes that needed coverage when teachers were absent. After a year or so, they offered him a full-time position as the In-School Suspension Coordinator. It was perfect! We were on the same work schedule and had the same holidays, snow days, and summer breaks. The girls loved that we were also on their school schedule for holidays, snow days, and summer break. It gave us a lot of traveling options for our family, without the hassle of any of us having to take time off from work or school for family trips or vacations. For the next few years, we worked together for the school district without any problems.

After Curtis's second year of teaching and my eleventh year, we started seeing articles in the local newspaper and on the TV news, that our school would probably be closing for good at the end of the school year. We did not know if it was a bad rumor or not, because the school that we worked for had said nothing about closing. Teachers did begin to talk among themselves about hearing that the school had asbestos issues, and did not have the funds to clean up the building, so they may have to shut down. Eventually, the principal called all the staff together into the cafeteria and announced that we needed to pack up the contents of our rooms prior to the summer break, because some programs would be moving to the high school before the next school year, but that some programs would come to an end, because there was no place to house them.

When Curtis and I realized we both would be out of a job, we started brainstorming of what we could do so that we both would be able to make a financial contribution to our household expenses. I was already fifty-two, so my options were limited. I had been in the cosmetology field for almost forty years as a cosmetology teacher and stylist. I felt as though I would be more comfortable staying in my lane. We talked about my possible options night-after-night, then concluded that opening our own cosmetology school would be the easiest for me. I did not want to go back into my home salon studio full-time, nor did I want to go work in someone else's salon as an employee. My legs and back were beginning to bother me from standing on my feet working as a hair stylist, from the time I was fourteen at my cousin, Rodman's salon. I did not feel like I had the longevity to work as a stylist, even though the money was good. So, we started looking at property around town that might be affordable for us to rent. We did not have any cash saved up for a project like that, but had lots of credit cards, as well as a few things we could sell to generate cash.

A few weeks after we had looked at three or four possible locations, I received a call at home while having a Memorial Day barbeque with my family. The school principal called me and said that the superintendent heard that my husband and I had been around town, looking at possible buildings where we could open a beauty school. I told her that was correct since we had been told that both our jobs would likely be ending in a few months. I explained that it was important that we started getting our ducks in order since both our incomes were necessary for our family financial obligations. Initially, I was concerned that the school district did not appreciate us, trying to put something together, while we were still employed by them. She explained that they were more interested in whether there was a possibility that we would be able to utilize our school to continue the education of their cosmetology students. She said, "What better place to send them, than with the teacher who has run the program for the last ten years." *Wow*! I was relieved. I thought we had jeopardized our jobs for the remainder of the school year. She asked if I would be interested in speaking with the superintendent after the holiday break. I immediately answered her with a yes. I spoke with Curtis, and we both thought it would be a great opportunity for us to get some guaranteed paid students.

When I returned to school after the holiday break, I gave the superintendent a call to discuss the conversation the principal and I had had over the weekend. She agreed with what the principal shared with me. She asked me if we had settled on a location yet? I told her no, but we were pretty sure that we were going to pursue the shopping center that was right across the street from the Vo-Tech school, where we were both teaching. She asked me a few questions regarding how many students we could enroll, the name of the school, our hours of operation, what we would be offering in our programs, etc. She told me it sounded as though we were moving forward, and would we consider looking at a building that was right across the street from the high school, that they leased before they completed the athlete house? She said, "If you are able to get that building, we could guarantee you fifty students a year."

She said it would work out perfectly for the district, because the students could walk across the street when they completed their morning academic classes. I agreed that it sounded like the perfect plan and would be a win-win for everyone. She gave us the name of the leasing agent and told me to get back with her after we looked at the building and discussed the terms with the leasing company.

After meeting with the leasing agent to see the storefront and discussing the details of obtaining it, before you knew it, we were ready to sign the lease. I reported back to the superintendent to make sure with her that if we leased the building, they were certain they would be sending their students. She told me there would be no problem, and that I should prepare for them to start in September, when the new school year began. She said they would be willing to give us an advance of $30,000.00 to order our books and supplies. We did not have the money we needed to lease the building, make the repairs, and order equipment and books, but we knew that if they guaranteed us fifty students, that equated to $250,000.00 a year; plus, we would be getting the advance, which would allow us to get started right away. I did the math over and over, because it sounded too good to be true, and because we knew how much they would be paying us. We sold our second car and got rid of a lot of bills. We cashed in our insurance policies, and took out a second mortgage on our house. We only needed about eighty thousand dollars to put it all together, and figured that if we went broke by cashing in our assets, it would be worth it, and would not last long. We knew that once we received the fifty percent deposit from the school district, we would be straight.

We decided to move forward with the project, and submitted the application and the first and last month's lease payment. It did not take long for them to approve our application, and give us the keys. I started ordering equipment and books using our credit cards, and Curtis started laying out the design for the classroom and student salon. He met with Jeff, the general contractor, who looked over what Curtis had put together, and simply made a few tweaks to his layout. He let us know the cost and the timeline to put it all together. It was already June, and we needed to be ready to open and start classes by September. We started working with the cash we had from liquidating our assets, but still needed the $30,000.00 advance that the school district promised to pay the general contractor, the electrician, the plumber, and a few labors that we needed to keep things moving. Because the store front was directly across the street from the school, they could see that we had began renovating the space. After a few weeks of working, the superintendent stopped in to see our progress. I let her know that we had not received the check for the advance, and had already depleted our on-hand cash. She let me know that it was in progress and that we would have something shortly. In the meantime, she had spoken with the Department of Education regarding the new partnership and requested they come visit our site to make sure everything was set for us to take the school district's students in September. They came for the visit, and spoke with Curtis and me. The Department of Education asked us several questions, and said that we could partnership with the school district as a satellite classroom, and reported the go ahead back to the superintendent.

After a few more weeks went by and we still had not received the promised advance from the superintendent, I made a few calls to her, but she did not return the call. I sent email after email, with no response from the superintendent. As we got closer to September, with a lot of work still needing to be completed, I began to worry that we would not be able to make the deadline for September. We had to stop the renovations because our cash had run out, and our credit cards were about maxed out. I kept calling and emailing, but never got a response. I even made a visit to the school district's administration building hoping to speak with her, but my visit was unsuccessful. I was told she was busy with the new school year about to start, but they would give her the message that I needed to speak with her immediately. A few more days passed when one of the teachers from the Vo-Tech told me that the school district's budget had been reduced, due to funding. They had to pull out of many of the projects and plans that were lined up for the upcoming year, and that they had heard we were one of them. I immediately felt ill and lightheaded. I thought I was going to pass out.

I went to the storefront that Curtis and I were putting together for our school, and told Curtis we had to talk. He could see the tears in my eyes and knew something was terribly wrong. I explained what I had heard, and he immediately said that that was the reason the superintendent was not returning any of my calls or emails. We had already invested everything we had into this project and had no money to complete the project or any students to start the program. It was a real mess. We did not know what to do or who we could call. We were too far into the project to go back to the leasing agent and pull out. We had signed a five-year lease. Equipment had been ordered and charged to our credit cards, and we were in the middle of renovations. Night after night, I cried and could hardly sleep or eat. I was beginning to feel depressed and hopeless. Curtis tried to comfort me by telling me it would be okay, but nothing worked to help me feel better. I was ready to throw in the towel. It was hard to figure out our next move because I could not get my mind off the fact that they led us to believe there was going to be a partnership, then threw us under the bus, with no notice or warning. It was hard to think or make a new plan.

Curtis thought it would be a good idea to get away for a few days to take my mind off of what they had done to us. So, we booked the next weekend at our timeshare in the Bahamas, that had already been paid for, and scheduled six months prior. We did not have any money, but we had enough open credit on our credit card to book round trip tickets. We started packing, and within a few days, we were in the Bahamas. We had already decided before we left that our mission there was not to be like tourists as usual, but to get with God. The plan was that we would do nothing, but stay on the resort, be still, and try to hear from God. The first morning there, we laid in bed, and for the first time, we watched a sermon broadcast with Joel Osteen. He was preaching about how God sends us signs to help guide us. He told a story about a lady and man who both believed in God and had both lost their spouses, who had been ill and died. These two got together and fell in love quickly. They planned to marry and had the support of their church.

But, the lady started feeling uncertain because it was so soon after her husband's death. She loved her husband and did not want to dishonor him or God by marrying too soon. At the last minute, hours before the wedding, the lady went to God in prayer and explained that she needed to feel like she had her husband's blessing, as well as God's, or she would call off the wedding. She asked God to send her a sign that she had their blessing. She wanted to be sure, and asked God to send her a rainbow, even though there was not a cloud in sight or any sign that rain was coming, as a sign to her that she had their blessing. Out of nowhere, there was a quick rain shower and when she opened the door, what did she see? She saw two rainbows, one from her husband, and one from God. She believed that was her sign to proceed with the wedding as planned. After hearing the message from Joel, I looked at

Curtis and said, "That's what we need: a sign to let us know whether we should move forward and try to open the school without the help from the school district, or whether we should call it quits and take the L."

Shortly after that, we decided to grab our morning coffee and take a stroll on the beach. While walking on the beach, Curtis pointed to a cloud and asked me what I saw. So that you understand, Curtis was one of those people who saw shapes in clouds. It could be anything from a bunny rabbit to a sports car, but I had become accustomed to it, and just kept walking. He grabbed my arm and made me stop and look. When I looked up, I saw a small rainbow, but it was upside down. He agreed that it looked like an upside-down rainbow. As we continued, the clouds stopped drifting to the right and opened at the location of the rainbow he had spotted. When the clouds cleared, it no longer looked like an upside-down rainbow, but it now went full circle, and what we thought was an upside-down rainbow was the bottom half of a rainbow-colored halo, hovering over the ocean.

As we looked at this thing hovering, more clouds cleared and what we thought was a halo turned out to be the bottom rim of a rainbow-colored crown in the sky. It was beautiful. While standing there studying the crown, I believe we went into some type of trance. It did not last long, maybe thirty seconds or so, but when it ended, he looked at me, and with excitement said, "Did you get it?"

I answered quickly, "Yes, yes, I got it. Crown Academy, that's the name for the school." I was so excited. Within seconds, all kinds of ideas and plans started shooting in our heads. The ideas were coming so quickly that we had to stop on the beach, borrow a pen and paper from a stranger, and start jotting down these ideas. They were coming fast; it was hard to keep up with them.

After about two hours of sitting at a table on the beach writing and brainstorming, my fifteen-year-old daughter and her friend came up to us and said they had been looking for us, and thought we were only going out for a short walk on the beach. We explained our vision of the crown and the messages God was sending us. I told them we had to finish writing and they could go to the swimming pool, and we would get with them later. My daughter assured me she was supposed to help with the planning, and did not want to leave us. I told her that it was not fair to her friend to sit with us, making plans. Her friend spoke up and said, "I think I'm part of the plan."

When I asked how she was part of the plan, she quickly said, "I'm supposed to sing at the grand opening," and that she wanted to stay with us too! My daughter asked what they could do to help. I told her that God had sent me a message that the phone number should spell the letters, "2 Divine," and that she could go on her computer, and find out how we would get those kinds of numbers. She worked on it all day, then reported back to us that it was called a vanity number, but that in our area back home, they were limited and there were no spots left for us. I thanked them for trying to help and that maybe I interpreted that message from God incorrectly. Curtis and I worked all week at the beach, researching things, and felt as though God was directing us to move on as planned. On the last day, Aynie came running to me and said that we had gotten the number I requested. She said something in her mind told her to check back that morning with the phone company. She said that when she had re-checked, she was told the number 234-8463, which was "2 Divine," with our local area code, was now available. She reminded me that I had given her the credit card number at the beginning of the week when she first checked in, and was able to use it to confirm the number for the school.

We were on fire, and so excited that on the next day, which was Sunday, we went to church and gave the testimony about our vision and how God worked with us all week, sending us ideas. I told my church that it was like God had said, "Oh! The school district dropped the ball; I need you to pick the ball back up and watch Me work."

Within a few days, people were calling us and said they had heard about our vision from their grandma, auntie, friend, etc., and wanted to be a part of it. In less than a week, we had the general contractor, a plumber, and electrician, all committed to doing the work and getting paid whenever we got the school up and running, but not worrying about the money now. They wanted to be part of God's plan for the school. We did not open in September, nor did we have any students registered, but God showed up and showed out. Before we knew it, we were invited to talk about our vision on a local radio station and a local television talk show. We gave every student who wanted to come to our school a $10,000.00

scholarship. We called it our Pioneer Scholarship, and since they were the first class, they only had to pay $5000.00; we allowed them to be on a payment plan with us, interest free. We opened our doors two months later with four students, but within thirty days of our first class, we had enrolled twenty-five students for the next class, and allowed the pioneer scholarship to be extended for one whole year. We were able to graduate more than forty students our first year. After a lot of praying, it turned out the school's name ended up being called Divine Crown Academy of Cosmetology, thanks to my sister, Marsha. The school was extremely successful. Not long after we opened, we were blessed to be able to branch the cosmetology program out to a nail technician program, an aesthetics/skin care program, a natural hair braider program, a barber program, and a cosmetology and barber teacher's program. We were one of the few, if not the only, school under our state board that offered every program that our state regulates. That rainbow was a sign to us: A sign that He was there to protect us from all harm and that our hope showed God that we have faith to continue to believe and look forward to the blessed life He wants for us.

> "Blessed is the man who remains steadfast under trial, for when he has stood the test he will receive the crown of life, which God has promised to those who love him."

> — James 1:12

Chapter 7

Weapons vs. Crowns: "Don't Let Anyone Seize your Crown"

The school had been open for a few months and was doing great! I had the help of Curtis, who had been enrolled as a cosmetology student. It wasn't in the plan, but he had a few renovations that he needed to complete, and our State Board of Cosmetology did not permit anyone, other than students, to be on the student salon floor during school hours. So, we made him a student, primarily so he could finish up the project and keep the school in compliance with the cosmetology school laws. It worked out quicker than expected, so he continued as a student and finished his hours, graduated, and received his license as a cosmetologist. Our daughter, Aynie, was the first student we enrolled. She had previously received her cosmetology license from working at fourteen-years-old as an apprentice at my salon, and received her cosmetology license at sixteen-years-old. So, when we opened Divine Crown, we enrolled her in our Teacher Program, which was a big help, because as a student teacher, she was allowed to work in the classroom and on the student salon floor. It was like having an assistant teacher.

At age seventeen, she received her cosmetology teacher's certification and was hired as our first teacher. Our daughter, Samara, was away at college, but helped at the school whenever she was home for the summer, or on a holiday break. She had also been enrolled in our Aesthetics Program, which she was able to complete while on summer break from college. I thought that was great! My whole family was working together. My sister, Marsha, even came on board. She had recently retired and told me that God spoke to her, and told her that she was to come work for us for free. I thought that was a bit much to expect, so we paid her minimum wage, and she was happy. It felt good, and seemed as though everything was perfect.

The school district's program at the Vo-Tech did not close as they had planned. Instead, after the teachers had been instructed to pack up the classrooms, once again the ball was dropped with their plan. They had no intention of opening the Vo-Tech building at the beginning of the upcoming year, and pretty much abandoned the building for the summer months. They honestly just left. They did not even close the windows or lock and secure the building properly. So, during the summer months, squirrels, birds, and other animals were able to enter the building.

They notified the teachers two weeks before that they were going back to the building, until further notice. I figured that since Divine Crown Academy of Cosmetology was not going to be ready to open in September as planned, that I would go back and teach as long as I could, or until the contractor had finished the job at our new school. They allowed teachers to go into the building a few days before the first day of school to prepare for the students to return. So, two days before school was scheduled to open, I went in to start unpacking all the boxes that they had us pack up when they told us they were closing, and that most of us would be laid off. When I pulled up to the building, all I could see was an unkept building. The grass had not been cut all summer. There was trash around the outside of the building, and some of the windows had been broken. It was not a good look, and I did not have a good feeling. I used my fob to enter the building and headed directly to my classroom.

When I opened the door to my room, I was in total shock at what I saw and what I was smelling. My room was a mess. I immediately screamed because there was a squirrel on the bookshelf. The second the squirrel heard my scream, it immediately leaped from the shelf to a desk to a window seal, then jumped out an open window. I looked around the entire area in disbelief at what I was seeing. There was bird poop on all the window seals, and it smelled bad. In fear of what I might find, I began trying to trace the smell. My detective work led me to the trash can next to my desk. My takeout Chinese lunch was still in the trash can from my last day. When I checked the other trash cans that the students used, they were the same. They still had the trash in them from the last day of the previous school year, which had been three months prior. There had been no cleaning of my classroom, and the boxes were exactly where I left them. Nothing had been done since my last day.

I worked for two full days cleaning the room myself and trying to get organized. It was August, and had been extremely hot that month. The two days I spent cleaning and unpacking, I was drenched when I left at the end of the workday. The school was old, and the building did not have air conditioning. I ran into a few of the teachers during those two days, and they all were complaining about how they had started making plans to start another job or were planning to sit back and collect unemployment for a minute. But, none of them believed they were coming back for the new school year. They all believed we were only brought back because the school district was not ready, and that if they had their ducks in order, we would have never been notified to return. It was Friday and school was scheduled to begin on Monday. I did as much as I could to get my classroom looking better than it did, then left for the weekend.

Monday morning came, and I dreaded going back to that place. I knew the students would walk in and be so disappointed. I woke up extra early to make sure as much as possible was in order. When the students walked through my door, they were so happy to be back, that they did not even notice that things were a little out of order. They all said they had missed me, and the new students were all excited to start cosmetology and have me as their teacher. I spent the morning going over the syllabus and talking about field trips. I was known as a teacher who took students on nice field trips. I had taken students to New York, Baltimore, and the Bahamas several times in the past. It was a nice morning. They did not even complain when I told them that they would not be getting their student kit, with the blow dryer, scissors, curling iron, etc., as well as their books. Neither of these things were at the school because of the late notice that we would be back in the old Vo-Tech building in September to start the new school year. It had started to get warm in my room, so I did not want to go too hard on the orientation. So, after a light morning of reviewing an overview for the year, students were dismissed for lunch. They were happy because it was starting to get hotter, and the cafeteria had doors that opened to the outside and was probably a little cooler than my classroom. Because cosmetology is a clock-hour class, it is considered a program, and the same students are with you all day and return to the same classroom after lunch. So, I would see them after lunch.

While the students were at lunch, I took the opportunity to unpack a few more boxes. After about a half hour of unpacking I noticed that I was a little lightheaded, so I took a short break to sit down and cool off. After feeling a little better, I continued trying to get as many boxes unpacked as possible before the students came back for the afternoon session. The next thing I remember is that I was lying on the floor, with students standing around me, yelling "Call the principal." Before I knew it, I was being carried out on a stretcher to an ambulance, and I remember asking the EMT what was happening. He explained that it looked like I was suffering from heat exhaustion, and was being transported to the hospital. They said that the students found me lying on the floor in my classroom.

That's when I got scared and said, "Please call my husband."

They informed me that he had already been called, and he would be meeting us at the hospital. When I arrived at the hospital, they checked me out and said I was dehydrated, and the heat in the classroom was ninety degrees. They checked my vitals and gave me an IV drip and oxygen.

Shortly after that, Curtis showed up and asked the nurse what had happened. They explained that the heat had gotten the best of me, but that I was fine, and could probably go home when the IV drip had emptied. The nurse came back in about fifteen minutes and said they were discharging me and that I should go home, drink lots of water, and get some rest. They suggested that I stay home the next day, because it was going to be another hot one. The district sent the students home shortly after I was taken away, because of the heat in the classrooms. In the two days I was home, all I could think was, *what if the students had not found me? What if it had happened later in the day and the students had already left? What if it happens again?* A lot was going through my head in those two days. Each morning, when I left the house to go back, I had a panic attack. I went to see the doctor on Friday, and I told him the entire story about coming back to the dirty, smelly, animal-infested classroom. I told him how the district threw us under the bus after we invested everything we had. He said he believed I was also probably dealing with stress. He suggested I take a few weeks off, get myself together, and see a therapist before returning to the classroom. So, that was exactly what I did. I had over sixty sick days and knew the time off would be covered, so I stayed home and relaxed.

As soon as I felt like I could exhale, I received a letter from an attorney saying that I was being sued by the school district. They dropped the ball, then threw us under the bus to fend for ourselves, and now they were suing me. I could not believe it. This was no joke; they were coming after me hard. They were charging me with several counts that could have my teacher's license revoked by the state board of cosmetology and the Department of Education. I was being charged with "Immorality, willful neglect of duties, and persistent and willful violation of, or failure to comply with, the school laws of the Commonwealth," all "based on the allegation that I misused the last of my paid sick days, and took part in establishing a business in the same occupational field as the school district, while taking leave." This was insane. They were not only trying to fire me, but they were also trying to *destroy* me. I did not understand how this was happening after we had had a vision with God, and He had given us that rainbow-colored crown while in the Bahamas. They called me in to tell me that if I would resign, they would drop the suit. They tried to tell me that I was playing sick, and getting paid for the time off that I was taking. They reminded me that to be a licensed teacher in our state, you must be of "good moral conduct" and that I was going to lose everything if I did not resign.

I was under so much stress from the district backing out of the promise to send us fifty students a year if we opened a school directly across the street from their building. During the short paid leave, I was sick, and I was under a doctor's care. But, instead of paying me for time off that I had earned, they wanted to steal my joy and take my crown. I said, "no," and called the union. They listened to my story and connected me with Attorney Scott. After meeting with him, he said he thought we had a case, and if we were ready for a fight, we could move forward with a counter-suit. Our suit would be to prove that the school district led me to believe we had a contract, even if it was only verbal.

Curtis and I agreed that we should fight their charges. If we won, all the counts against me would be thrown out, I would get all my sick pay, as well as doctor's visits paid, and they would list me as being laid off, not fired. By the time we filed the counter suit, the Vo-Tech had finally closed as planned. The talk was that the building was old and had a lot of asbestos throughout the building, and that they did not have the money to have it removed, so they had to close. With the school now being closed, if we won, they would have to list me as being laid off. And, if the school opened back up, they would have to call me first and give me the option to come back to my same teaching position.

Once we got started, it seemed like a long process of meetings with the attorney, letters going out, responses coming in, and finally, a hearing. Honestly, the hearing was the most difficult and had to be broken into two different dates. It was hard because I only had a few witnesses and the school district lied like crazy. They tried to say they never spoke with me, nor made any promises to me. Their claim was that it was all in my head, and that I stepped out on my own, hoping they would send students. Unfortunately, I had dozens of emails between me and the superintendent, a phone call log that went on for weeks, as well as pictures of them visiting our school, while it was being renovated.

They met with us to check and see if we met the regulations and guidelines of the State Board of Cosmetology and the Department of Education. I had documentation from the hospital and my doctor that stated I was under a lot of stress, and I was being treated by him for stress/anxiety with medicine, and seeing a therapist weekly. All things were presented at the hearings as evidence by my attorney. All they had were lies and hearsay, nothing concrete. At the conclusion of the second hearing, my attorney let me know there would be about a ninety-day wait for the verdict. He said the judge would look over all the evidence presented, before making his decision. Ninety days went by and there was nothing from the judge about his decision. I'm sure I called the attorney every week after the ninety days, asking if he had heard anything from the judge. He told me, "Sometimes, it takes a little longer and that it's good the judge isn't rushing to make the decision. That means he is taking his time looking over our case."

I was sure I was getting on his last nerve with the weekly calls. Honestly, the wait on the decision was driving me crazy. I was so afraid the state would revoke my license for immorality if I lost the case to the district's claims.

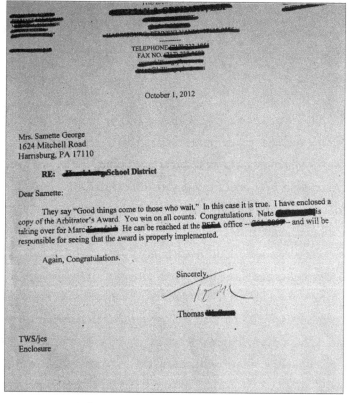

TELEPHONE ████████
FAX NO. ████████

October 1, 2012

Mrs. Samette George
1624 Mitchell Road
Harrisburg, PA 17110

RE: ████████ School District

Dear Samette:

They say "Good things come to those who wait." In this case it is true. I have enclosed a copy of the Arbitrator's Award. You win on all counts. Congratulations. Nate ████████ is taking over for Marc ████████ He can be reached at the ████ office -- ████████ -- and will be responsible for seeing that the award is properly implemented.

Again, Congratulations.

Sincerely,

Thomas ████████

TWS/jcs
Enclosure

Letter from our attorney, with the judge's decision.

After about five months of waiting for the judge's decision, I received a letter from the attorney. I was so nervous, I could hardly open it. I'll never forget the first two lines of his letter to me. It read, *"They say 'Good things come to those who wait.' In this case, it is true. I have enclosed a copy of the Arbitrator's Award. You win on all counts. Congratulations!"*

I called Curtis and read it over and over again. God did not leave me hanging. They were not going to take my teaching credentials, and Divine Crown was going to be fine. It felt so good. Divine Crown was a big success, and as years went by, it got to the point where we had a waiting list to enroll. Our daughter, Aynie, became the first teacher we hired, and by our fourth year, she had been promoted to school supervisor. We had decided to start preparing for her to take over the school when we retired, or at the least, make sure her credentials were strong enough to find a job running someone else's beauty school. We were blessed to retire and sell the school to our daughter, Aynie, a few years ago. She was the perfect choice, since she was there from the beginning of the vision. She even hired her sister, Samara, to take my place as the school's compliance officer. We now only act as consultants to the school. Truly, we serve an awesome God.

> "Behold, I am coming quickly! Hold fast to what you have, that no one may take your crown. He who overcomes, I will make him a pillar in the temple of my God, and he shall go out no more."

> — Revelation 3:11-12

Chapter 8

Sickness to Death:
"Bad News"

As time went by with the success of the beauty school, we moved our location to a larger building in a more diverse area, and added barbering to our list of programs. We started discussing the possibility of retirement. I was already sixty-two years of age, and had close to fifty years in the cosmetology field as a teacher and hair stylist. Curtis was fifty-eight years old, and we spent the last twelve years operating our school together. We were both starting to get tired and saw that these new millennial students were much different than the type of students we enrolled in the beginning. I guess it boiled down to me not wanting to retrain my brain to deal with them. They were all great students, but not as receptive to my style of teaching, which was making it much harder for me. Curtis saw that I was starting to get discouraged, and agreed that retirement should be in our near future, while we were still young enough and healthy enough to do some traveling and see a bit more of God's beautiful creation.

So, we decided to put out feelers to see if we could find an interested buyer. We spoke to several people who were interested. But, either they could not secure financing, or they realized that without us, there would be too much of a learning curve, as well as a lot of hard work and little-to-no profit their first few years. Once our daughter, Aynie, saw the possible sales fall through, she came to us and presented the idea of her buying the school. We thought it was a great idea, and offered to stay in the background as consultants. She had already been a teacher at the academy for ten years and our school supervisor for the last eight years. She was only twenty-seven, but we felt confident that she could do the job, plus we were there to help her out. After months of working with SBA for funding and planning for a settlement date, it all fell through. When she shared with us that they had told her it would not be a go, it seemed like the worst news in the world. As for the best laid plans...

Based on everything we had been told by the SBA, we had moved forward with our plans to retire and this new information about Aynie's funding falling through was a real bummer and a monkey wrench in our plans. She too had started making plans, and spending most of her savings to move forward as the new owner. We were all devastated and did not know which way to turn. We only had a few weeks left to make our plans work, but knew a new buyer would not be able to put the purchase together within a few weeks. There were several documents that had to be submitted to the state board of cosmetology, the U.S. Department of

Education, and an accreditation agency. The process to purchase a school takes several months to get an approval to be an owner, so I knew it wasn't going to happen with a new buyer. After the three of us did some quick brainstorming, we came up with a solution to move forward with selling the school to our daughter. She did not have much money, but was willing to give us everything she had. And, she promised that in a few years, when her school started generating a cash flow, she would help us out with our finances and pay off our house, which was one of the things we had planned to do with the proceeds. Before we turned the school over to her, we emptied its operating account, which was enough to live off of for several years. So, despite our initial plan with cashing out on the sale, things worked out. She even hired our other daughter to take my place as the compliance and officer manager. It all allowed our legacy to continue, which was a beautiful thing.

A few weeks before the settlement was final, Curtis received a diagnosis of having Stage 2 prostate cancer. We thought that we would be retiring soon, and now there was this news. We had just come off of a forty-day surrender fast with a great group of believers and felt as though the fast had prepared us to deal with this crisis. We met with several doctors for their opinions about the best way to tackle this new challenge. We spoke with a radiation oncologist, a chemotherapy oncologist, surgeons, and one nut who was a naturals doctor who told us, in the middle of the country's Covid pandemic, that it was okay to take off our masks at his practice, because he believed there was no such thing as Covid, and that he would never recommend the vaccine to any of his clients, because it was merely the government's way of shooting healthy people with cancer-causing agents. When I asked him if he believed in God, he said that sometimes he got God to assist him. We could not get out of that place soon enough. It took a minute to find the right doctor who made us feel comfortable. We prayed about it, and within one week, several people, such as our accountant, one of my clients, and one of our daughter's employees brought up Dr. Owen's name as one of the best in the field of prostate cancer. So, we decided to give him a call.

Unfortunately, his receptionist said that he was not taking on any new clients for the next five months. It felt like we were back at square one. I made a call to our accountant, who was a friend of the doctor, and asked him to put in a good word for Curtis, then asked him to please consider working with him as a patient, which he did. A few days later, Curtis received a call from Dr. Owens's receptionist, who said that the doctor had a cancelation, and if we could make that one-and-only appointment, he would see Curtis. We felt truly blessed, and Curtis was so pleased that he agreed to the date and time.

When we walked into his office and saw a Bible on his waiting room coffee table, we believed our prayers had been answered. When we sat down with Dr. Owens, it was clear that he was our guy. We told him how we had been searching for the right doctor and told him about our recent encounters. Before he even examined Curtis, he told us he was a Christian, and that he would have his wife put Curtis's name on her prayer group's prayer list. He seemed knowledgeable, and suggested the procedure to remove the prostrate before it moved into Stage 3. Because Curtis had a brother pass away a few years back from prostate cancer, and had another brother who was currently battling Stage 4 prostate cancer, Curtis and I made the decision together to move forward with the surgery. The day of the surgery, we felt confident we had made the right decision. After the surgery, the doctor came out to the waiting area to speak with me concerning the procedure, but I was on my knees praying, so he decided to give me a few minutes and come back. When he returned, the first thing he said was that the Holy Spirit was in the operating room. He said that he prayed before surgery, during surgery, after surgery, and that his wife's prayer group had been praying as well. He said that it was almost unbelievable, that he performed the surgery and there was hardly any blood. He was sure it was nothing but God. After surgery, I was already waiting for Curtis in his room. He was in good spirits, and said he was not in much pain. He did great and three days later, the doctor discharged him from the hospital to go home. Praise God!

One week later, Curtis had to go back to the doctor's office for a short visit to have the catheter and some other drainage tubing removed. On our way back home from the doctor's office, I asked Curtis what he wanted for lunch before putting him in bed to rest, and to continue healing. He said that because he had been on a lite diet the first week, he wanted me to make him some good old-fashioned deep-fried chicken, and requested that I did not make it in the air fryer the way I usually do. After parking the car, we went across the street to checkout and help with an issue my neighbor, Jill, and her husband, were having with hanging their TV. Curtis was going to give them a few pointers and suggestions before going into our house and going to bed.

I knew I no longer had a deep fryer, but remembered my mother-in-law deep frying chicken in a large pot with cooking oil, so I figured I would do the same thing. Once we got back to the house and I got him settled back into bed, I started preparing his lunch. I pulled out a big pot like my mother-in-law, and filled it with cooking oil. As I was waiting for the oil to get hot enough for me to drop in the chicken, I decided to water my herb garden on the back porch. I had neglected them from spending so much time at the hospital and being Curtis's nurse maid for the first week that he was home.

As I was watering my plants, I saw Jill in her driveway, and we began to chat. During the short update conversation we were having, her husband began to yell from his porch that Curtis was calling me. I told him that he probably wanted to know how soon his lunch would be ready. He said, "No, he is yelling and screaming."

I thought that maybe he fell trying to get out of bed. When I turned around to go back into our house, I looked and saw smoke coming out of every nook and cranny of our home. As I ran back into the house, I saw Curtis in the kitchen, and the entire stove was on fire. He had gotten the fire extinguisher, and was spraying foam on the fire, but it was not helping. The fire began to spread from the stove to the microwave above, then to the cabinetry and ceiling. I yelled out to my neighbor, Jill, to call 911 and have them send a fire truck to our house. I never saw a fire up close and had no idea how quickly it could spread. While waiting for the fire truck, Curtis was still trying to battle the fire alone. At first, I could see his full body, but then the smoke began to get blacker and blacker, and he began to fade out of my sight. When it got to the point where all I could see were the bottom of his legs, I yelled for him to get out right away before he was overcome by smoke. As he stumbled out of the house, we could hear the siren from the fire trucks coming. We lived at the base of the mountain, and there were no fire hydrants in our neighborhood, so the fire company only had the water that they carried on the trucks. When they arrived, they immediately pulled out the hoses and started spraying the kitchen. They did not have to use all their water, because Curtis had got most of the fire out with the fire extinguishers that neighbors started bringing to the house. It took about fifteen minutes to put out the fire, but afterward, there were a few hot spots, where small fires started up again. After about an hour, they told us it was all out, but that it was not safe for us to stay in the house, because of all the fumes from plastics burning. They said they had to shut off the electricity and gas, and that it had to be checked by those departments before we could stay in the house. There was nothing we could do at the time, but to check into a hotel. Thank God we had insurance that covered the hotel stay. We stayed at Samara's the first night, and we checked into the hotel the next afternoon. We ended up being there for sixty-two days, while the kitchen was reconstructed, and the entire house and its contents treated for smoke damage. I could not believe that I burned down our kitchen in our new house that we had only been in for fifteen months. But, we felt blessed that no one got hurt. We missed being in our new home, but were in a comfortable long-stay hotel, which was like a small apartment. It offered free breakfast every morning, and hot coffee and tea twenty-four hours a day, which Curtis loved. It felt like home and there was even enough room that our granddaughters, Kya and Kali, who I called my "lady bugs," could still come stay with us on the weekends. It had a swimming pool and a nice outdoor area, so they looked forward to coming to our temporary home.

Unbelievably, the third week we were there, we were awakened at 7:15 a.m. on a Sunday, with a call. They said there was someone on Facetime Live videoing a bad car accident, and that it looked like our property where our daughter leased her three-story beauty salon and a small barber shop. I immediately called Aynie and told her what I had heard. We had their daughters overnight, so she and Kyle were able to quickly get dressed and head to the property. Curtis threw on a sweat-suit, and headed to the property to meet them. By the time he headed out the door, I began to get calls from friends asking me if I'd seen what was on Facebook. I didn't have Facebook, and told them, No, but Curtis had headed out to the property and was going to call me soon as he got there."

About a half hour later, Curtis called me and said it was bad. He said a car missed the turn on the road and crashed into the barbershop on one side, and came out on the other side, then continued through the courtyard and crashed into the salon. He said it looked like a bomb had gone off. My daughter called shortly after and was crying. She said that the entire barbershop had been demolished by the car crash, and that the salon was in bad shape. She said there was a car that was crushed, but there was no driver, and that maybe someone saw the accident and took the driver to the hospital. She said that the fire trucks, police, and ambulance had arrived, and were all assessing the accident. She said that I needed to get there as soon as possible, and that Kyle would come pick up the "lady bugs," and take them back to their house, so I could go to the property. About twenty-five minutes later, Kyle came and picked up the girls and I headed to the property. When I pulled up, I could not believe my eyes. There were people everywhere: TV news trucks, fire trucks, ambulances, and police taping off the area. Truly, it looked like a war zone.

Car accident at our daughter Aynie's barber shop on our property.

Car accident at our daughter Aynie's salon on our property.

After a few hours of the police checking the barber shop and salon for loose electrical wires and gas leaks, one of the police officers called out, "I see a hand." There were piles of bricks on the porch of the salon from the car knocking out the pillars in the crash, so you could hardly even see anything on the porch. Come to find out, when they started pushing away the bricks where they saw the hand, there was a full body of a dead woman. All that time that everyone was on site, they never knew that the driver was dead and buried on the salon porch under tons of bricks. My daughter had to witness them finding her and carrying her away. She was devastated. She had recently installed a security camera three days before the accident, and was asked by the police to view the footage. It was terrible and something that still haunts her today. Aynie was able to witness the entire accident. The footage showed the car coming through the barber shop at over 100 miles-per-hour, then hitting the salon at top speed, and the young lady being expelled from the car onto the salon porch. The security camera timed the accident at 5:30 a.m. early Sunday morning, but was not reported until 7:15 a.m. Thank God it was a day when the barber shop and salon were closed, or there would have probably been more fatalities. If it would've been the day before and a little later, there would have been men, women, and children coming into the salon, maybe even my daughter who started working at 6:00 a.m. Most days, she came in early to prepare for her first appointment. It was bad. Because that evening was Trick-or-Treat, the police said the area had to be cleaned up quickly, because children would be passing the property, and it was a safety hazard. Friends and neighbors in the community stepped in and helped clear the bricks away so that children would not be in danger as they passed that evening. They cleaned up the bloody bricks, so she could also enter the salon to see the damage inside. Once the bricks were moved, there was lots of blood that took days of scrubbing to remove. When the investigation was completed, we were told the driver was going 101 mph, with a BAC of .214%. The legal limit in Pennsylvania was 0.08%. It was reported that they had found an opened alcohol container in the car. Unfortunately, drinking and driving do not mix. The report said she died on impact, and was a wife and the mother of two children. The salon and barber shop were closed from November until June for reconstruction, renovations, and repairs. We were sorry for the loss of the young woman, but grateful that no one else was hurt.

> "Praise the Lord, my soul and forget not all of his benefits, who forgives all your sins and heals all your diseases, who redeems your life from the pit and crowns you with love and compassion."

> — Psalm 103:2-4

Chapter 9

The Battle Has Begun:
"He Can Do the Impossible"

T hings had began to look much better for us. We had moved back into our home, which had been renovated and cleaned up from the kitchen fire. The barbershop and salon had also been restored from the car accident, and looked better than they had ever looked. They both were opened back up for business and my daughter started acting like her old self again, which was great. We decided to celebrate by taking a mini-vacation to Florida, and arranged for my "lady bugs" to go to Disney World. It was a great weekend getaway. Unfortunately, when we tried to return, we ran into a delayed and canceled flight nightmare. Curtis and I went on the trip to help Aynie and Kyle with the lady bugs, but we ended up getting separated on different flights on the return trip home. We decided that since they had the little ones, it was best for them to take the first available flight out, and Curtis and I would be on standby for the next flight we could get back home. We ended up sitting at the airport for hours before finding out that the next available flight for us would be the next day. We located a nice Air-BnB to stay at for the night, and found food to take back to the spot. By the next morning, I was coughing a lot and was having chest pains. We boarded our flight on time, but because we were separated from my daughter and her family, we had no transportation to get back home from the airport. So, we had to Uber approximately 120 miles to get home. It was an expensive ride, but it was our only option. By the time we arrived home, the coughing and chest pains had gotten worse. Curtis insisted that he take me to the ER at our local hospital to get checked out. The way I was feeling, and the symptoms I was having, led me to believe I had probably picked up Covid. So, off to the hospital we went.

When we arrived, due to the chest pains, they gave me an EKG to rule out a heart attack. They also thought that I could possibly have had a pulmonary embolism from sitting on the plane for such a long time, so a CT-scan was ordered, along with a chest x-ray. Curtis's sister had just passed away suddenly, with no signs or symptoms, from a pulmonary embolism only three weeks prior, so I knew how serious that was. They gave me something for the pain while we waited for the test results to come back. After about an hour, the doctor came in and informed me that I was not having a heart attack, nor did the tests show the possibility of a pulmonary embolism, which was great news. He told me what the x-ray showed was that I had pneumonia, which was causing chest pain and the cough. He gave me a prescription and said to take it easy and rest for a few days, and I would start feeling better in a week or two.

After three weeks went by and I still had the cough, I called my primary physician, Dr. Gerlach, and informed him that the ER had diagnosed me four weeks prior with pneumonia. He said he had access to their records and would pull the results from the test they ran, and get back with me shortly. About an hour later, he gave me a call and said that I may have had pneumonia, but that the x-ray showed a definite mass on my left lung. He said he would arrange for me to see a lung specialist immediately, and to watch for his office to reach out to me to schedule an appointment.

Sure enough, the next day I received a call from Dr. Moritz's office. His nurse said he wanted to speak with me as soon as possible and asked if I was available to speak with him through a virtual appointment the next morning. I said, of course, and we agreed on a time. I told Curtis about the scheduled appointment and asked him to sit in with me. The next morning, I followed the instructions sent to meet with him virtually. When his face appeared on my laptop screen, he introduced himself to us, and said that he had spoken briefly to Dr. Gerlach about my test results. He agreed that after reviewing the test results that there was a definite mass on my lung that concerned him, and the only way to know exactly what it was, and to rule out cancer, was to perform a biopsy as soon as possible. Curtis and I discussed the procedure with him and agreed to having the procedure done four days later. Prior to surgery, he met with me after I had been prepared to go into the operating room. He explained how long the procedure would take, and reminded me that he would be taking a sample of the mass, as well as brushings from both lungs, and performing an ultrasound. He informed me that it would take a few days to get the pathology report back from the samples, but his nurse would reach out to me to schedule another virtual appointment. I had no problems with the biopsy procedure and was discharged shortly after waking up in the recovery room.

That evening, I did a lot of coughing up phlegm and assumed his procedure broke up whatever the mass was, and that I was coughing it up. The next morning, I was breathing better than I had in weeks and was no longer coughing. Five days later, we met again, virtually, but because I was feeling so much better from coughing up so much phlegm, I told Curtis not to bother with joining me for the appointment and to go support Stew at the racetrack. I told him I was going to work the day of the virtual appointment, and would meet with Dr. Moritz in between clients. When it was time to call him for my afternoon appointment, I excused myself from my client, who I knew would be under the dryer with a roller set for at least forty-five minutes, and I made the call.

When Dr. Moritz came on the phone, he asked how I had been feeling since the biopsy, and had I had any problems after the surgery? I explained that I was feeling much better and that whatever he did must have loosened that phlegm on my lungs, and that I was breathing and feeling better. Very forward, with no beating around the bush, he said, "I understand what you're saying, but the test indicates that you have Stage 3 lung cancer that is spreading, and you don't have much time."

I was shocked and asked him if he was sure he was speaking to the right patient, since he only had met me face-to-face one time, which was prior to the biopsy surgery. He held up my report and said, "Is this you, Samette George, birthday of November 24, 1958," and I think he pointed to a small picture of me in the top, right-hand corner. I felt like I was in a tunnel and what he was saying was muffled and unclear. I said, "Please stop, I'm not sure I heard correctly."

He repeated himself, and this time he added that it was spreading fast. He said that based on the size of the mass the x-ray showed that the ER had taken seven weeks ago, it was much larger now. He said, "It needs to come off right away, but it is too large to operate on and we need to shrink it first. I will have my nurse start setting up tests to see if we should go with radiation or chemotherapy to shrink the mass." I knew right then that I was in a battle. He told me I would hear from his office in a few days, after they set up testing schedules and appointment times. When I received the bad news, I was alone, and I had to go directly back into the salon to finish Ms. Van's comb-out. When she saw me, she asked if I was ok. She could see in my face that something was terribly wrong. As soon as I finished, I called Curtis and explained Dr. Moritz's report. Curtis said he had just got to the racetrack, but was turning around and heading straight home, though it would take an hour or so. She was my last appointment, so I was able to leave right away. Unfortunately, I was so frazzled that I locked the salon, but left my keys inside, which had the salon key and my car keys on the ring. I had to ask Ms. Van's son Herbie to give me a ride home. We had been the best of friends since childhood, and he too, knew something was not right with me, and agreed to give me a ride.

I had only been home fifteen minutes before my doorbell rang, and it was both my daughters standing in the doorway with a sad look. It was strange that they rang the bell, when they both had the code to the house and had never rang the bell before. I immediately assumed Curtis had called them, since he knew it would be a while before he got back. They both came in and sat down, when Samara began to cry. I knew then that Curtis had spilled the beans. I looked at Samara and Aynie, and said, "It's going to be alright, but please no tears, just prayers."

We talked briefly, but I told them that I did not have much information, only what the doctor told me, and that we would know more after all the tests were completed. They sat with me until Curtis called and said he was ten minutes away, then they left. Samara had an appointment with a client at the salon and Aynie had to pick the girls up from daycare. But, as she walked out the door, she had an epiphany, and looked back at me and said, "Mom, I'm supposed to share my breast milk with you. It will help your immune system." That's exactly what she began to do from the first surgery, through the chemo treatments, and until after the last lung surgery. I believed it was all part of God's healing plan.

Once Curtis arrived, he walked into the house, immediately came to me, and gave me a big hug for a long time. We discussed what the doctor had said, and thought it was best to give our pastor and my sisters a call first thing the next morning and let him hear the bad news from us. My sister, Marsha, told me, "Not to worry, we will put it in God's hands, who is the Great Physician."

My sister, Stevie, told me not to accept that diagnosis into my heart or my spirit. We called our pastor and explained what we had been told by the doctor, and he immediately said, "We all need to fast and pray." Pastor Dockens suggested that we ask family members and friends to join us. He said he would put together the plan, as well as reach out to a few church members and invite them to fast with us. He said that once the plan was together, he would reach back out to us so we could share the instructions with those who were going to participate with us. He called us the next day, which was Friday, and said that we should do a seven day fast by praying half-hour in the morning for strength, followed by only drinking juice during the day, and the evening would consist of an additional half-hour of prayer for healing, and only eating fruit. We agreed and began the fast on Monday morning. I had never prayed half-hour straight, and thought that would be the hard part. But, once Curtis and I got started, it was so much easier than we thought. We prayed so hard that we got so caught up in the prayer, and before we knew it, a half-hour had passed, and we were looking forward to my fruit juice concoction recipes. In the evening, I was able to get creative with the fruit-only dinners. I learned that string beans, peppers, tomatoes, eggplant, avocados, peas, cucumbers, olives squash, nuts, corn, pumpkin, and sunflower seeds are all fruits. So, I was able to make some wonderful dishes that I would have never known about, if it was not for the fast. The fast, with prayer, went from Monday morning until Sunday at midnight. It made my body and mind feel great. I was so proud that we were able to complete it without complaining. One thing I knew for sure was that we were going into battle. Thank God that the Word made it clear that the battle was not ours, it was the Lord's.

> "So we fasted and implored our God concerning this, and He listened to our entreaty."

> — Ezra 8:23

Chapter 10

Something Like Job:
"Yet Another Messenger
of Bad News"

After seven days of serious praying and fasting, I woke up the morning after the fast had ended, with tears in my eyes. It appeared that I had been crying in my sleep. As I began to put a little thought into why I would have been crying, I remembered that I thought I had a dream. But, the more I thought about the dream, it was more like putting the pieces of a puzzle together. The thought of the dream got clearer and clearer. I dreamed that God spoke to me in the dream. I started to remember exactly what He said to me. I didn't remember seeing anyone in the dream, but remember a man's voice, that was crystal clear when He was speaking. I could no longer hear anything, but I could feel Him still speaking to me. He said, "Sam, this is not about you, but all about Me. I need to use you to shine my light through as a beacon to draw others to my kingdom. There are still too many who don't believe I am on the throne and still in the miracle-making business."

Wow! Immediately, I knew it was not a dream, and that God had spoken to me in my sleep, and I was still feeling Him speaking when I woke up. I began to cry again and believed that it was the real thing. I knew that God had chosen me for a serious task. I believed that out of all the people in the world He could have picked, He picked me. Right away, I felt honored and blessed. I knew He was going to see me through the Stage 3 cancer diagnosis. I knew at that moment I had to open my mouth and start telling everyone I could about how God spoke to me. I was so excited when I told Curtis, and knew I had to let others know that God was still on the throne, and was going to heal me. It made me feel beautiful with no worries. He made me feel like I was His favorite and had nothing at all to worry about. I knew He was simply using me, and it made me feel so special.

A few days later, I began taking lots of tests for Dr. Moritz, so he could determine whether we should be looking at chemo or radiation to shrink the mass on my lung. We also met with a few oncologists for their opinion on what should be our next move. The first oncologist we met with said that depending on how far into Stage 3 it was, it may not be curable, and their only goal would be to extend my days, but not to cure me. That doctor seemed to be very knowledgeable, but *not* encouraging. When I asked if they believed in God, with a proud voice, she said, "Sorry, No God." I knew she was not the doctor to lead the team to help me. I immediately called

Curtis's doctor, who helped us with the prostate cancer diagnosis, and asked for a referral for a faith-based doctor. He said that I should ask to be referred to Dr. Reninger. I called Dr. Mortitz's office and explained how we felt about the meeting with the oncologist, and that we needed to be switched to Dr. Reninger. We met with him that week and knew right away that we wanted to work with him. He told us we could call him Dr. Chip if we liked. I continued to call him Dr. Reninger, while Curtis preferred Dr. Chip, or just Chip. I asked him if he believed in God, and he quickly said, "I don't do anything without the Big Guy upstairs." He assured me that he would do everything he could for me, and that he would meet with us again after all the testing was completed.

Curtis and I were so burned out from processing the Stage 3 lung cancer diagnosis, as well as beat from the testing all week. I had to undergo an MRI, a PET scan, ultrasound, a pulmonary function test, and lots of blood work. When I thought I had caught pneumonia from sitting around the airport months before, we decided that we would get an RV motor coach. We thought that by avoiding public transportation and hotels, it would cut down on our chance to contract Covid and everything else that was floating around in the air.

We also met again with my primary physician, Dr. Gerlach, for a follow-up appointment. He knew I had been taking tests all week, and asked if we had spoken to Dr. Reninger since the tests had been completed. I told him that I did not. He suggested that since the last of the results came back a few hours ago, that if we did not hear from him in a day or two, we should give him a call. I told him we would, and we headed home to get ready for our weekend adventure. We were excited about leaving, especially after that brutal week of testing. We were finally heading out on our first trip, the shakedown. We had filled the refrigerator, loaded up our baggage, and crossed out everything on our checklist. We were minutes away from heading out for a Labor Day weekend, and were looking forward to picking up our friends, Denise and Denis, at the airport, who flew in from Florida to join us. We were all going to be heading to Virginia to meet up with the AARVC, an RV group that we had just joined. Minutes before we headed out of our driveway, we received a call from Dr. Reninger. He did not say he had spoken with Dr. Gerlach, but I was sure it had something to do with the call. He asked if Curtis was around to join us. I called Curtis into the house and let him know that Dr. Reninger was on the phone.

As soon as Curtis came in, I let the doctor know that he was on the speaker phone, followed by Curtis hollering out a greeting. He asked how I was feeling, then went right into letting me know that the test results came back, and that I did not have Stage 3 lung cancer. He said, "You have Stage 4 lung cancer, and it has already spread to your brain, so you will need to have emergency brain surgery." He told me that the mass on my brain had to be removed immediately, because the tumor was in an area where I could literally wake up blind or worse. He said I did not have much time and that he had already spoken with the neurosurgeon, and his office would reach out to me immediately.

I asked him, "How soon do I need to get this done?"

He said, "You need to see the neurosurgeon tomorrow, and he will schedule the surgery to take place in the next few days."

I said, "Are we talking about brain surgery, where they operate on my brain?"

He answered, "Yes, that's what I am saying."

I looked at Curtis, and he looked at me, shaking his head in disbelief. I explained to Dr. Reninger that we were heading out for the Labor Day weekend for some R & R, that we badly needed. He suggested that I stay and meet with the neurosurgeon, but I said no. I told him that God had spoken to me, and that God would keep me over the weekend, and I would be ready to meet with surgeon on Tuesday. He said that if I was definitely going to leave the area, he would need to prescribe anti-seizure medicine, just to be on the safe side. He told me to take it easy and that he would speak with me after I met with the neurosurgeon. We made a call to my sister, Marsha, and a call to Pastor Dockens, to give them the update, and we headed out to pick up the anti-seizure medicine and our friends at the airport.

When we pulled in, we could see our friends, Denise, and her husband Denis, waiting for us under a pavilion. We stopped directly in front of them and could see the smiles on their faces. They had no idea of the bomb I was getting ready to drop on them. Once they were settled into the RV, Curtis took off and headed straight to the highway for our four-hour drive to Virginia. I didn't want to hit them with the bad news right away, so we chatted for about five minutes about our expectations at the campground. After our chat, I made them a drink for the road, and told them that we needed to discuss something now, so that we could get it out of the way, and get on with our vacation. They knew that I had received the Stage 3 lung cancer diagnosis and had participated in the fast. I explained that God not only spoke with me at the end of the fast, but that the fast gave me direction, and strengthened me for what I was about to tell them. Right away, Denise aske what it was that I needed to discuss. Without hesitation, I told them that as we were heading out the door, the doctor called with the latest test results. I explained the lung cancer had metastasis to my brain, which took my cancer to Stage 4 lung and Stage 4 brain cancer, and that the chance for a cure was unfortunately unlikely. They were both speechless and could not even open their mouths. I reminded them that God had spoken with me, and that I was only being used to draw others to His kingdom, and am not accepting or receiving that I am in that category of "unfortunately, unlikely." I told them that we were to carry on, as though we'd never heard the update. They both looked a little sad, but I quickly told them, "No tears, just prayers." We discussed it briefly and moved on.

I spent most of the ride down contacting my appointments for the next two weeks, canceling or rescheduling them with other stylists. I did not want to wait until the last minute. I knew it was inevitable that I was going to have brain surgery, and wanted to give them a heads-up courtesy call or text. Hours later, we arrived at the camp group and met up with

Curtis's two buddies, Eric and Stew, who caught up with us in Stew's RV, and drove down behind us. We had planned to park the two RV's directly next to each other, with our entrances and awnings facing each other. The plan was to create a larger space for us all to cook out, play music, and party.

But, once we arrived, I insisted that we not park together. Stew and Eric were a little bummed out by the new unspoken arrangements, but I was not feeling like a big four-day party. It was late when we arrived, so there was enough time to set up the RV, our camp area, and eat dinner, before turning in for the evening. I did not want to talk about the diagnosis while on our weekend getaway, but I thought I owed Eric and Stew an explanation about why I requested us to be separated at the campground. They both were supportive and recalled that I had told them that God had spoken with me and told me that this was not about me, and that I was merely being used. We had a great time that weekend, and spoke little about what I was up against as soon as I returned home. While we were there, I received a call from Dr. Eseonu, the neurosurgeon's office. They set up an appointment for me to come in for an office visit on Thursday to meet with the doctor.

Once we were back and settled, we made a few more calls to friends and family members. We called our daughters first and gave them the update. I did not want to share the new bad news with them while we were on the road. I knew it would spoil their weekend and they would be thinking about me the entire time we were away. For me, it was important that people knew I was okay and believing and trusting in what

God had said to me. I was afraid that if I did not speak up, rumors would start traveling that had been twisted about my condition. So, I wanted as many as possible to hear it from the horse's mouth. To this day, I'm not sure if that was a good thing or bad thing. So many people tried to tell me what I should be doing. Many could not understand why I was going to stay in our small town, with small-time doctors, to have these major operations. Some told me I should be heading to Johns Hopkins since we were only hours away. Some questioned why I was not going to Hershey Medical Center, which was only twenty minutes away. Some thought I should be heading to Philadelphia, which was only an hour-and-a-half away. Then, I had a stranger insist that I go all the way to Texas to MD Anderson, one of the leaders in cancer treatment. I had to explain over and over again that God had spoken to me and that He was only using me. I had to let them know that wherever I went, God was going before me, so it really did not matter. I could tell by the look on many faces that they thought I was crazy or in denial. Curtis and I had discussed all these possibilities and decided that we were staying with our UPMC team of doctors. It just felt right.

We headed out on Thursday to meet with Dr. Eseonu for the first time. The receptionist welcomed me to his office and a nurse led Curtis and I back to an examination room. When the doctor came into the room, the first thing I noticed was that he was very young. He greeted us and we greeted him back. Then, I immediately asked, "How old are you?"

He answered, "Thirty-eight." He must have felt my concern, because he quickly said, "Brain surgery is what I do all the time." He let me know he was a graduate from Johns Hopkins University. Before he went any further, I asked him if he believed in God. Without hesitation, he said, "Of course I do."

I knew then that we were in the right place, and felt extremely comfortable with Dr. Eseonu. He told me that he had already looked at my test results, as well as met with Dr. Moritz and Dr. Reninger, and they all felt like the tumor should come off to extend the days I had left. He let me know that he was confident he could remove the cancerous tumor. He gave me a light neurological examination and asked me several questions. He could not believe that I never had any signs or symptoms of having a brain tumor. He further explained that most of the tests that were run were when the other doctors thought it was only lung cancer. But now that it had metastasis to the brain, he would be performing surgery on my brain to remove the tumor. I needed several other tests to be performed right away, so that he could see more clearly what he would be working with during the procedure. He also informed me that he had never performed brain surgery on someone who did not have any signs or symptoms, such as headaches, seizures, blurred vision, dizziness, passing out, stumbling, or ringing in the ears. I told him my story about how God had spoken with me and had told me that He was only using me. And, I had not and would not accept the diagnosis into my spirit. He let me know that he had scheduled the brain surgery for the following Wednesday, which would give us enough time to have many of the first tests repeated, but more so, concerning the skull area. We understood, and in the next three days, I had to undergo several more tests to prepare for brain surgery.

Tuesday evening, prior to surgery, I received a call from Dr. Eseonu. I answered the phone and once I confirmed that he was speaking with me, he asked if I was still feeling good and if I was ready to move forward with the brain surgery the next morning. I answered, "Yes, I'm all prayed up and ready."

He said that he had just received the results of the last test results, and that it looked like my spine had been compromised and I needed to have spine surgery as well. He said he did not like to perform two surgeries on someone on the same day, so he took the liberty to reserve the operating room one week after the brain surgery to correct my spine, but would discuss it with me in more detail the next morning before the brain surgery. I felt like I was going to pass out. I quickly called Curtis to the phone and asked Dr. Eseonu to please repeat what he told me to Curtis. While he was speaking to Curtis, I saw a small tear in his eye, and he shook his head in disbelief. When we got off the phone, we decided that we would not call and tell the girls yet, and would wait until after the brain surgery to share more bad news with our friends, family, and Pastor Dockens. It had been a long day for us. That evening, my daughter, Aynie, had given birth to our new granddaughter, Khloe, which to me was the best news in the world, and then we were hit with a bomb. We had to be at the hospital by 6:00 a.m., and I was hoping to get there early enough to meet Khloe for the first time on the maternity floor. So, after the call, I double-checked my hospital bag, took a shower, and went to bed. I called my big sister, Marsha, and she reminded me of the Book of Job, and how a messenger came to him with bad news and before they left, another messenger hit him with more bad news, and before that messenger left, still another messenger with more bad news. With everything that had come against him, he refused to curse God. Instead, he still believed in God's Word. I felt the same way. Nothing was going to separate me from the love of God. I still felt honored that He had selected me to use for this incredible task.

> "Though He slay me, yet will I hope in Him; I
> will surely defend my ways to His face."
>
> — Job 13:15

Chapter 11

God Went Before Me:
"He Blessed Their Hands"

Early the next morning, we slept until the last minute, then got up and headed directly out. I was not allowed to eat or drink anything after midnight, prior to surgery, so I did not want to have much time in the house after getting dressed. Curtis and I discussed the night before, that once they took me back to the operating room, he would grab his coffee and breakfast. We arrived about twenty minutes early, because I wanted and needed to get a glimpse of my newest "ladybug," baby Khloe. When I arrived at the hospital, they registered me, gave me my arm band, and directed me to the surgical waiting area for further instruction. I told the receptionist that I needed to go to the maternity floor first to visit my new granddaughter. She told me that since the Covid pandemic, they tightened up the restrictions, and only the father could go on that floor outside of visiting hours. She said it was only patients, nurses, and doctors who were permitted this early. I looked at her and reminded her that I had an armband, indicating that I was a patient, and gave her a big smile. She smiled back and said, "Okay," and directed me to the maternity floor elevator, saying, "Give it a try." So, that was exactly what I did.

Curtis and I went directly to the eighth floor where Aynie and the baby were roomed. We quickly went past the nurse's station and into Aynie's room. She was so happy to be able to see me before surgery, and passed Khloe straight to my arms. I got teary-eyed when I saw our brand-new baby girl. She truly made me feel good. I got to hold her for about five minutes, then took the elevator down to the seventh floor to the surgical waiting area. As soon as we entered the area, they said they had been waiting on me, and thought I had gotten lost. I told them there was an angel on the eighth floor who I had to meet before surgery. I explained that baby Khloe was born the night before, and she smiled.

She told me someone would be out for me shortly, and that once I was dressed and ready for surgery, Curtis would be brought back to spend a few minutes with me before they rolled me into the operating room. Shortly after they had me put on a surgical gown and gave me the IV drip, they brought Curtis back. We talked, prayed, and listened to a few gospel songs. Then, the entire surgical team began to come into the room. They all introduced themselves and explained what their job would be once we were in the operating room. Their conversation with me was helpful and relieved much of the anxiety I was feeling.

The entire UPMC team was phenomenal. The last to come into the room were the anesthesiologist and the surgeon.

The anesthesiologist told me the technique he would be using to put me under, then he had me sign a few papers, and asked if I wanted something to relax me before they took me back to the OR. I said yes, and he put something in my IV, then said he would see me in the operating room. I had been carrying my vision board around, which was a board my friend, Stephanie, suggested that I create to help me with my journey. It was a dry erase board, and had a scripture at the top that read, "And the God of all grace, who called you to His eternal glory in Christ, after you have suffered a little while, will himself restore you and make you strong, firm, and steadfast. To Him be the power forever. Amen," (1 Pet. 5:10-11.)

At the bottom, there was another scripture, that read, "Heal me, Lord, and I will be healed, save me and I will be saved, for you are the one I praise," (Jer. 17:14.) I had been carrying it around from the beginning of the diagnosis and explained that I wanted to make sure that we were all on the same page. I asked the entire team to sign it, and I was so happy that they all agreed to sign it. In fact, I asked everyone at the hospital and doctors' offices who had anything to do with my testing, my treatments, or my surgeries, to sign it as well, and no one turned me down.

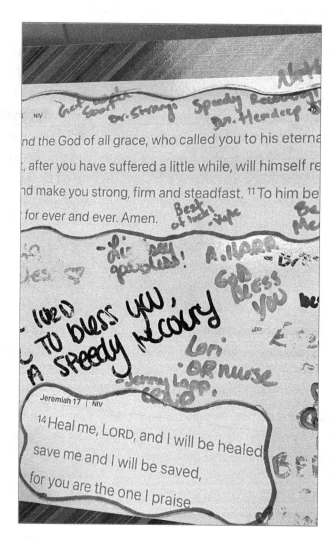

My Vision Board, with everyone's signature in my healing pathway.

Lastly, Dr. Eseonu entered the room. As promised, Dr. Eseonu quickly pulled up my x-ray and explained the situation with my spine. He told me it was an underlying condition, and that it had to be corrected. He said he took the liberty of reserving the operating room the following week to come back for spinal surgery. I knew he believed in God and asked if I could pray over his hands. He told me that would be fine. The pre-surgical instructions made it clear that there was to be no lotions, oils, deodorant, makeup, hair gel, or hair spray, used on the morning of surgery. What Dr. Eseonu did not know was that I had put anointing oil that my friend, Mary, had brought back from Jerusalem between the webbing of all my fingers before the surgical team came into my room. So, when he thought I was holding his hands praying, I was anointing his hands for the brain surgery. But, I knew it had to be done, so I did it. After I anointed his hands, I prayed for everyone on the surgical team, and for God to take control and orchestrate the entire event, from beginning to end. Then, Curtis reached over, kissed me, and said he loved me. Wow! All I could think of is that in a few minutes the doctor would be sawing off my skull to operate on my brain. All I could say was, "Thank you, Jesus." As they rolled me into the operating room, I sang "How Great is Our God, until I feel asleep.

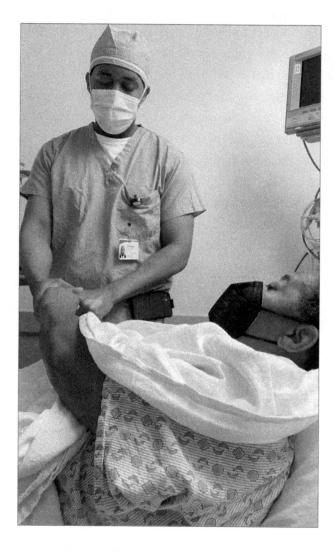

Praying and Anointing Dr. Eseonu's Hands.

When I woke up, I was in the recovery room. They asked me if I knew my name, knew where I was, and if I knew why I was there. I answered their questions, and they took me to my ICU room. When I went into the room, Curtis was already waiting for me. I could see that he had purchased and hung a picture/quote on the wall by Erma Bombeck that I admired in the gift shop, and used often when I spoke. It read, *"When I stand before my God at the end of my life, that I would not have a single bit of talent left, and could say, I used everything you gave me."* It was a wonderful surprise. Curtis asked me how I felt, and I told him I was good, and not in any pain. I told him I was hungry and told him to call the nurse to ask if I could have something to eat. When she came into the room, she said I had to be on a light liquid diet for my first meal, and that she would place the order. Shortly after she left, a young lady brought me some broth, Jell-O, and an iced fruit cup for dessert. It did the trick, and felt like it was enough. Curtis stayed with me until they kicked him out at about 10:00 p.m. Visiting hours ended at 9:00 p.m. The nurses came and checked on me and my vitals every single hour and all through the night. It was a little annoying and I got no sleep, but I knew it was necessary.

The next morning, Dr. Eseonu came in bright and early to check on me. He asked me how I was feeling, then gave me a neurological test. He said I was doing great, and could start on a regular diet. He was amazed at how well I was feeling, and how well I was managing the pain. He took off my head bandage and said that the physical therapist would be in shortly to work with me, and then he left. The physical therapist came in about 8:30 a.m., and explained that they would be working with me, but that they had already planned for me to spend two weeks at a rehab facility to work on my speaking and motor skills. They asked me lots of questions, then took me on a walk around the hospital floor. They were surprised that I was walking as normal, and wasn't having any words in my speech slurred. They told me to take a few more walks when Curtis came, and to try to keep talking as much as I could. They told me I was doing remarkable.

Curtis came back to the hospital around 10:00 a.m., and we took another morning walk around the hospital floor. He stayed until I fell off for an afternoon nap. Then, he came back at 5:00 p.m. to walk with me again and stayed until 9:00 p.m., when the visiting hours ended. Samara came down after work and they allowed her to bring Aynie down from the maternity floor in a wheelchair, but not with the baby. We had a great visit, and they were so happy to see me up watching a movie. They knew how much I loved a good movie. My appetite was not the greatest, so Curtis normally ate half of my meals. That second night, the nurses did not come in as much, so I was able to get a better night's sleep than the first night.

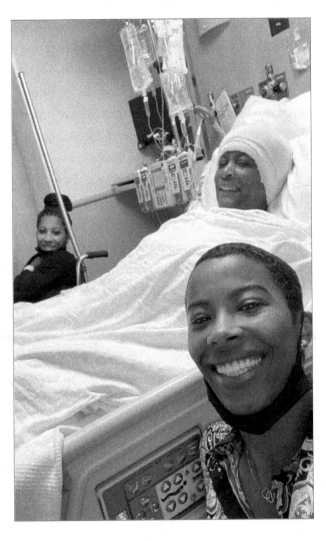

Me with a visit from my daughters, Samara and Aynie,
after Brain Surgery.

My daughter, Aynie, who was on the floor above me with the new baby, called me at 7:00 in the morning, and told me that God had spoken to her in a dream, and told her that there was someone on my floor I needed to pray with that day.

When I asked Aynie who, she said she did not know. When the breakfast attendant brought me my breakfast, I asked her if she knew of anyone on the floor that needed prayer. She said she would check. Dr. Eseonu was in my room bright and early to check on me; he gave me the neurological test again and said I was doing great. The physical therapist came in while he was there, and said that I passed all their tests. Before they left, I asked if they knew of anyone on that floor that I could pray with in their room. They said, "No." When I questioned that there must be *someone*, they answered no, again. They reminded me that I was on the cranial floor, and that most patients on that floor recently had brain surgery. They told me fifty percent are on life support, many are in a vegetative state, and the others are in no condition for a visit. They told me that I was the only patient on that floor who was eating on their own, and able to walk around.

When the physical therapist came in and examined me, they said they were canceling the two weeks scheduled at the rehab, because I had already met the expectations needed to be released from the rehabilitation facility. Dr. Eseonu came back and said he was signing my discharge papers, and that I could go home. Wow! I could not believe it. Aynie had a baby on Tuesday, and I had brain surgery on Wednesday, and I was leaving the hospital before she was discharged. All I could say was, "Thank you, Lord."

I started packing my things up right away. When Curtis came into my room and saw me sitting in a chair with my bag next to me, he could not believe it. I had put my makeup on and a cute cap, and was ready to go. Right before we left, the breakfast attendant, Briana, came back to pick up my lunch menu. I told her that I was being discharged, and asked if she had located a patient for me to pray for before leaving. She said, "No." I explained that I promised my daughter I would find the person before I left the hospital and pray with them. She assured me there were no patients whose room I could enter. I explained that God told my daughter that that person was on the floor with me, so please think hard. She looked at me and began to cry, and said, "It was me."

I said, "you?"

She explained that she was very young and pregnant, and felt as though she was going to lose the baby because of all the stress she was under. She said she was hoping to get a better response and support from her family about the pregnancy, but it did not happen, and she found herself crying all the time. I prayed with her before she left, and reminded her to look to God for the strength she would need to get through the pregnancy.

We left the hospital; we made one stop at the grocery store to pick up my prescription. I was feeling good, so while we waited for the medicine, I did a little shopping. When we arrived home, I did not feel like going to bed, so I didn't. I felt great and had planned to cook dinner, but instead, Curtis's daughter, Sheena, and my grandson, Greyson, stopped by and dropped off dinner for us to eat. We talked for a while, ate dinner, took a shower, and turned in for the night. For the next few days, I felt normal, so I followed my normal daily schedule at home, as if I never had the surgery. For the most part, ice and Tylenol kept the small degree of pain at a tolerable level, which was about a two. My head was looking crazy after the cut Dr. Eseonu gave me to perform the craniotomy, so four days after the surgery, I went to the salon and had my friend, Chris, cut all my hair off. He did not understand why I wanted him to cut my hair days after brain surgery and while there were staples still in my head. He said "No", but I insisted. I knew that a cut would make me look better, and feel better. He did an excellent job and I thanked him. Before I knew it, I was starting pre-admissions testing all over again for the spine surgery that was scheduled in a few days.

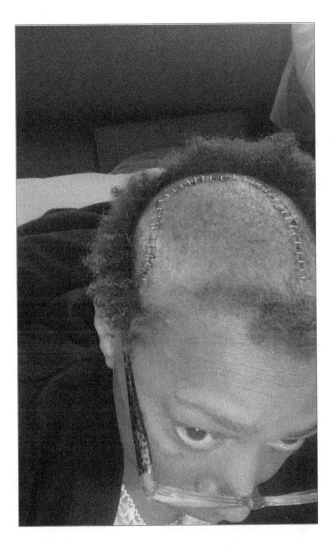

Crazy cut Dr. Eseonu gave me prior to brain surgery.

Completed hair cut by Christoper O.

The following Wednesday came quickly, and we headed back to the hospital. I was scheduled for spinal surgery at 8:00 a.m. When I arrived, they took me back to start preparing me for surgery, then brought Curtis back to stay with me until it was time for me to be taken to the operating room. Like before, the entire surgical team stopped into my room and introduced themselves to me. They all told me what they would be doing in the OR, then left. The anesthesiologist had me sign his paper, then left to join the others. Dr. Eseonu came into the room and asked how I was feeling, then reminded me of the procedure he was going to perform, as well as the technique he would be using. He let me know that to get to the vertebrae that was the problem, he would have to cut my throat to get to the spine area. He said he did not expect any problems with the surgery, and that he would meet me shortly in the OR. Then, Curtis gave me a kiss, and told me that he loved me. The nurse rolled me away while I recited Psalm 23, until I fell asleep.

When I woke up, I was in the recovery room, and they were preparing to take me to my ICU room. When I arrived at my room, Curtis was there waiting. It felt good to see him. I asked him to get me some ice to suck on since I was not able to eat. The nurse had already told me that I would not be able to speak for a week, and would need to drink slushies or smoothies out of a straw for a few weeks. So, I knew ice was all I was going to get the first few hours. They brought me broth, and a ginger ale for dinner, and an icy fruit cup for dessert. I had no pain at the location of the incision, but I was achy in my shoulders. So, the nurse brought me a few heat packs to help with the pain. That night, I had to sleep sitting up, but it was fine. The next morning when I woke up, the first thing I was concerned about was whether I could talk. I tried to say a prayer, and it came out crystal clear. So, then, I videoed myself singing Stevie Wonder's "Knocks Me Off My Feet," but changed the words to "But, God, I love, I love you, I love you," and sent it to my friend, Denise.

After a while, she called me laughing, and wanted to know how I went into the hospital for brain surgery, had my throat cut for spinal surgery, and woke up singing like Whitney Houston. We both laughed and laughed and laughed. Then, when they brought me in my breakfast, I assumed it would be apple sauce or something pureed, but instead, when I took the dome off the plate, I saw bacon, eggs, and French toast. I was sure they were not aware of my diet after having my throat cut. I used the call button to signal the nurse to change my meal. But, I was so hungry that I took a small piece of French toast and balled it up, and sucked on it before swallowing, and it went down smoothly. I tried it again, then a third time. When I saw that I had no problem or pain eating, I continued, and by the time the nurse came in, the food on my plate was all gone.

Plate of breakfast after throat and spine surgery: eggs, bacon, and French toast.

Empty plate–I was not supposed to be able to eat solid food for one to two weeks, but I cleaned the plate.

Later that morning, Dr. Eseonu came in to check on me. He asked me how I felt, and if I was in any pain. I told him there was no pain, just achy shoulders. He said that the soreness was from how they had me positioned to perform the actual spinal fusion. He was amazed that I did not have a sore throat, and had no problem talking. When I told him I just got done eating a full breakfast of bacon, eggs, and French toast, he smiled and said, "Great!" He told me that the pathology report had come back from the tumor he removed from my brain. With amazement in his eyes, he said that the report confirmed that the tumor was not cancerous. He said, from the MRI and CT-SCAN, it showed all the characteristics of a cancerous tumor. He apologized, and said he was sorry that he gave that diagnosis. But, because there was no cancer found in the brain, my Stage 4 diagnosis had been downgraded to Stage 3 lung cancer, which was treatable. All I could think about was how that late in the midnight hour, God turned it around. All I could say was, "Thank you, God."

Dr. Eseonu said that he was going to sign my discharge papers, and that I could leave as soon as the nurse went over the homecare paperwork. Curtis arrived shortly after the doctor left. When he saw me packing up, all he could do was smile. He apologized for not bringing me the smoothie he had promised, and said he planned to bring it back that afternoon. I accepted his apology and said, "Take me home." We made one stop at the grocery store to pick up my prescription. I was craving chicken wings, so I did a little shopping, and when we got home, I cooked us dinner. Curtis said he felt bad that I was cooking dinner minutes after I was discharged from having surgery the day before. But, I explained to him that I felt like I wanted to cook. After dinner, I showered and prayed, then went to bed. I had to sleep sitting up the first few nights, but was grateful that I was able to come home the day after surgery, and sleep in my own bed. In fact, a year before, after the fire, we had to get a new mattress. Curtis had found a good deal on a sleep number bed that was much like a hospital bed and allowed me to sleep sitting up, with no problem. To this day, I never knew why we bought that type of bed. God is awesome.

> "The Lord goes before you; He will not leave you nor forsake you. Do not be afraid; do not be discouraged."

> — Deuteronomy 31:8

Chapter 12

Good Medicine: "Poison is Toxic, But God Makes it Work"

A few weeks had gone by, and I was feeling like I never had surgery. My hair had already grown back from the doctor shaving my head to perform the craniotomy surgery. The scar on my throat from the spinal fusion had completely disappeared, as if I were never cut. My next few appointments were back with Dr. Reninger, the oncologist. On the first visit back, he was happy to hear how well both surgeries went, and surprised, like the other doctors, that what they thought was a cancerous tumor turned out to not be cancer. I'll never forget him sitting down with us, and him pulling out a sheet of paper that said their goal would now be to cure me, not merely extend my days. I could tell he felt genuinely happy to point to their goal on paper. He told me they would reach out to the department that would schedule the port implant procedure, and they would be in touch with me as to where and when it would take place. He explained that the port would help simplify the IV Drip for the chemotherapy sessions.

Dr. Reninger discussed the two chemotherapy medications I would be receiving, as well as the one immunotherapy medication that I would also be receiving at the sessions. He discussed, in detail, the pre-meds that I would get and let me know that I would be there from 8:00 a.m. to 4:00 p.m., hooked up to the IV drip. I told him that everyone told me I would be putting poison in my body. He agreed that it was toxic, but they would be monitoring me with blood work at each session. His nurse, Dana, told me that I could experience hair loss, fatigue, nausea, vomiting or weight loss. I told them that I didn't plan or expect to experience any of those things. I told them that God was only using me and that He promised this would not be a hard thing for me. Dr. Reninger told me that they would start with three sessions every twenty-one days. He said that their plan was to shrink the mass to be small enough that it could be surgically removed by Dr. Moritz in three months. He asked if we had any questions. Both Curtis and I shook our heads and I said, "If we come up with any, we will give you a call." He told me they would start chemotherapy after the incision from the port implant healed, which would take about two weeks.

One week later, I received a call to set up the surgical procedure for the port implant. Within a few days, Curtis took me back to UPMC hospital for the procedure. I met with the doctor, and she explained how the procedure would be performed, and assured me that it would take less than forty-five minutes. She told me I would be getting twilight sleep, which would relax me, but that it would not take me completely under, but I would feel no pain. Sure enough, the procedure took less than one hour, and I was able to leave the hospital minutes after having the procedure. It took about two weeks for the implant to heal, and it felt sore and itchy for about three weeks.

Once the soreness subsided, my first chemo treatment session was scheduled. I went for my treatment every twenty-one days as I was told by Dr. Reninger. I was a little nervous at the first treatment. I had prayed that the treatment would not make me sick or nauseous, as I was pre-warned by the doctor, and all the literature they gave me to read. The nurses in the chemo room were so welcoming, pleasant, and friendly. They checked on me constantly to see if I was comfortable, and to make sure I did not need a snack or something to drink. I took my phone, which I loaded up with lots of Netflix movies, and had a journal to write in that my new friend, Elli, gave me as a gift. She was my own personal support team. Elli was a lung cancer survivor for more than twenty years and a real inspiration on my journey. I arrived for my first treatment at 8:00 a.m., and before I knew it, eight hours had passed, and they were unhooking the IV drip from my port. I went home about 4:00 p.m., and then had a twenty-one day wait until the next treatment, but did not have one single side effect during that time. I felt blessed. At the next treatment, I was told that the second treatment was the one that normally started thinning or baldness, but once again, I had no side effects.

The only sad part of my second treatment was that I met up with Chef Cassy, a good friend of my family. I did not realize that he had been lying next to me all day, but before leaving, I recognized his voice. He looked good and was in good spirits, but had lost enough weight that I did not recognize him. He had been our personal caterer for several of our celebrations. I went over and prayed for him, told him to keep the faith, and reminded him that God was still in the miracle-making business. The last treatment was the same as the other two, except this time I got to ring the bell, which indicated I had completed my treatments. It was a proud moment for me. Dr. Reninger and the staff were so happy to see me celebrate.

Me ringing the chemo bell, with Dr. Reninger and his staff.

"And these signs will accompany those who believe: In my name they will cast out demons; they will speak in new tongues; they will pick up serpents with their hands; and if they drink any deadly poison, it will not hurt them; they will lay their hands on the sick, and they will recover."

— Mark 16: 17-18

Chapter 13

The Breath of Life: "Finally, My Lung"

Three weeks after my final chemotherapy session, and my bell-ringing celebration, I returned to the hospital for another biopsy of my lung with Dr. Moritz. He was checking to see if the chemotherapy was effective, and had shrunk the mass through the treatments. After he checked my lung, he could determine the steps that he would take to remove the mass. The biopsy went quickly. This was now the fifth surgery, and registering me into the hospital was the same procedure as all the other surgeries. Once the nurse dressed me for the procedure, Curtis was allowed to come back and stay with me, until they rolled me away. The surgical team all introduced themselves and let me know what their job would be in the operating room. Last was the anesthesiologist, with his paperwork, followed by Dr. Moritz, who recapped what would happen during the procedure. He would see me in his office once the report came back from the pathologist. Afterward, Curtis kissed me like before and said he loved me. I had spoken with my god-daughter, Shannon, the day before, and she requested that this time I sing, "What a Mighty God We Serve," until I fell asleep, which is what I did.

When I woke up, I was in the recovery room. The nurse asked how I was feeling, and if I needed anything. I told her that I felt fine, but my throat was dry, and I requested for her to bring me some ice chips to suck on. Shortly after, she left the room and Curtis walked in with a big smile and kissed me. Right after that, the nurse came in with my ice, went over my discharge paperwork, and said I could leave. We stopped and got some take-out Pho, then went directly home. We ate the soup, then relaxed for the evening with a movie before turning in for the night. A few days after the biopsy, I had a few more tests I had to take before seeing the doctor again. Four days later, Curtis and I returned to Dr. Moritz's office to discuss the results of the biopsy. During our meeting, he let me know that he was happy with the results. He let me know that the mass on my lung had shrunk from 4.0 by 3.6cm, to 3.1 by 2.6cm, which was now small enough to remove. He also let me know that the SUV or strength of the cancer, and the ability to spread, had weakened. It had gone from 10.4 to 4.6, which was great! He said that the tumor board had met and discussed my case, and they agreed that, based on the test results, we should move forward with surgery the following week.

The doctor let me know that they would be performing a lobectomy. He explained that the left lung had two sections: an upper lobe and a lower lobe. He reminded me that the mass was attached to my lower lobe and that he would have to separate it from the upper lobe to remove it. Dr. Moritz was a robotics surgeon, and described how the device would enter my body, separate the lobes, then pull out the lower lobe. He went on to tell me that after reviewing all the scans, he noticed that I have a strange anatomy, which was called a, "not uncommon." He told me that the left lung normally had just two sections, but that my lung showed an extra section, or a third lobe. So, once he removed the lobe with the cancerous mass, I would still have two lobes left, like most people. He told me that he could not explain the third lobe. I quickly said, "I can. Look at God! Sixty-five years ago, when God planted me in my mother's womb, He gave me an extra lobe for a time such as this." Honestly, it gave me the chills just thinking about how God worked.

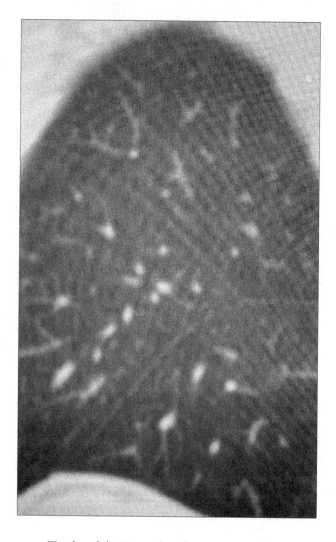

The three-lobe X-ray, when the norm is two lobes.

He instructed me to have another pulmonary function test, as well as an echocardiogram, a few days before the big lobectomy surgery, and that he would meet with me the morning of the surgery. All the tests were performed and indicated that my lungs and my heart were strong enough to handle the removal of almost half my lung. He told me to expect to be in the hospital five to seven days after the surgery, then we left and went home.

Six days later, it was the morning of the big surgery. We had been preparing sixth months for the lobectomy. Curtis and I got up extra early so we could do our morning study of the Word on the Bible App, which we had been doing every morning since Curtis's prostate cancer diagnosis. When we arrived at the hospital, the registration for surgery was the same as the previous five surgeries. The nurse, Milly, a friend from church, registered me in, then signaled another nurse to take me back, and I was dressed for surgery. Curtis was brought back so we could spend a few minutes together before being taken back to the OR. The surgical team came into my room and introduced themselves, followed by the anesthesiologist and Dr. Moritz. After speaking with Dr. Moritz about the procedure, for the first time throughout this entire journey, I shed a few tears. I knew this was the main surgery, and what we had been planning for sixth months. I knew that the risks were much higher than the previous surgeries. When Curtis saw me crying, he came over, gave me a big hug, and said, "God got you," then gave me a kiss, and told me he loved me.

After that, they rolled me back as I sang "Victory is Mine," until I fell asleep.

When I woke up, I was in the recovery room, with a nurse next to my side. She asked me how I was feeling, and if I was in any pain. I told her I felt fine. Shortly after asking me a few more questions, she took me to my ICU room, where Curtis had been waiting. Soon as they got me settled, Curtis came to me and kissed me. We were so glad to see each other and started conversing immediately. We both were in awe that I was not in any pain, and that I was able to walk to the bathroom on my own. I decided that I did not feel like lying in the bed, so he got me a pillow and I sat in the reclining chair. We discussed how God had showed up, showed out, and in my case, showed off. An hour went by, and the nurse brought my dinner. She told me to try to eat a little and see how my stomach handles the food, before eating a lot. I was so excited about how good I felt that I did not listen to their instructions about eating light. I ate all the food, and immediately threw my dinner back up. Because I vomited, I was told I had to get into the bed. I should have listened. Once I was settled in bed, Curtis gave me a kiss and left to go home. It was a long day for him, and I knew he was tired and ready to go to bed.

The next morning, the nurse woke me up early and told me I was scheduled for a chest X-ray at 6:00 a.m. So, I got up and as soon as I finished in the bathroom, I was wheeled down to the lab to get an X-ray of my lungs. Once I returned to my room, I had my breakfast, and thank God, this time it stayed down. At about 9:00 a.m., the respiratory team came in to check my breathing, and to give me two devices to do breathing exercises with to help keep my lungs clear. They were surprised that I was breathing so well, and so soon after lung surgery. I was instructed to use the devices every hour, and they said they would come back in an hour to check on me. When the respiratory nurse came back to check how strong my breathing was with the exercise device, he was amazed. He said my breathing was as good as his breathing. Dr. Moritz came in at about 10:30 a.m. to check on me. He asked me how I was feeling and if I was in any pain, or having a hard time breathing. I told him, "I feel great; I was not in pain, and my breathing was fine."

He told me that my X-ray looked good and that the nurse would be in my room shortly to remove the drainage tube and my catheter. He said once that was completed, I could go home. He said he did not see any reason to keep me in the hospital, and that I could go home and rest. Dr. Moritz told me to take it easy, and that the only restriction he was giving me was that I was not clear to drive. He said that I may have trouble turning my body, and would probably feel sore under my arm until the incisions healed. He told me that I did not need to go to bed, and I should try to walk as much as possible. He assured me that the surgery went fine; he did not expect any complications, but to continue the breathing exercises, and that he would see me in his office in two weeks. I could not believe that twenty-four hours after having half my lung removed, I was discharged and soon would be heading home.

When Curtis came in and saw me packing up, he shook his head in disbelief. I looked at him and said, "God is good; take me home." I was texting praise reports before we pulled out of the hospital parking lot. Like with the other surgeries, we stopped at the grocery store to pick up my prescription, and did a little shopping. Afterwards, we went home, and I cooked dinner. My daughters stopped by for a brief visit to make sure that I was good. Afterward, we found a movie to watch in bed, said our prayers, then went to sleep. I woke up the next morning, praising God. He told me he was only using me, and He had kept His promise. Truly, He is the Great Physician.

Curtis and I going home the morning after lung lobectomy surgery.

"The spirit of God has made me, And the breath of the Almighty gives me life."

— Job 33:4

Chapter 14

Because He Lives: "Faith Can Heal"

I t had been ninety days since the lobectomy, and I felt great! I definitely hadn't felt like half my lung was removed. I have been back to the oncologist, as well as my surgeon, for a follow-up on two different occasions. Each time, more tests were run to check my lung, spine, and brain, as well as the rest of my body. Dr. Eseonu, Dr. Reninger, and Dr. Moritz all agreed that there were no signs of cancer in my body, and that there was no need for any type of post-surgical treatment. They said there was no need for any more chemo, radiation, or medicine, because there was nothing to treat.

I constantly reminded all my doctors that they did an awesome job, but that God was the Great Physician. I loved all my doctors and nurses, and believed that God would bless them for being obedient. Dr. Eseonu, Dr. Reniger, and Dr. Moritz were the best! I thanked them from the bottom of my heart. They all allowed me to pray with them, and knew that I was asking God to orchestrate everything they did. Truly, I believed they all were assigned by Him, and believed that the first two oncologists — the one who said, "Sorry, no God," and the other who said, "no cure, but we will try to extend your days," — were not assigned by God. So, right away, they were pushed out of my pathway. Once God lined up His team, there was no stopping them and their plan to make me whole again.

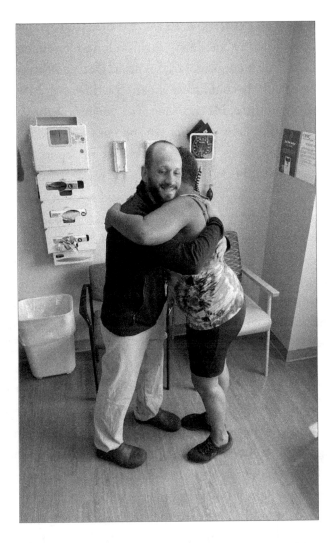

Me giving Dr. Moritz a big thank you hug at my post-surgery follow-up
appointment.

I truly believe that a major part of my healing was my faith, and my doctors agreed. From the time God had spoken to me and said to me, "Sam, this is not about you, but all about Me," I felt honored. I felt so special that out of everyone in the world He could have chosen for this assignment to let His light shine, He chose me. The assignment for Curtis and me was to show our strength and faith to lead others to His kingdom, where they too would have an opportunity to inherit eternal life. When God gave me my assignment and told me He was only using me, all I could say was, "send me." From that moment on, I refused to be shaken or pulled away from what I believed was a promise from God. I wanted, and believed, that I would be like the woman with the issue of blood. For years she suffered, but when she knew Jesus was coming through her town, she believed that if she could only touch the hem of His garment, she would be healed. It was her faith, trusting and believing in Jesus, that healed her. I felt the same way, that if I could touch Him, I would be healed. I believe that the fasting and praying touched Him, and that is why at the end of the fast, I woke up with tears in my eyes, knowing God had spoken to me. I trusted and believed there was another report. I was determined not to let the test results or doctors' reports sway me to the right or left. I was going to stand on His promises and nothing less.

Jesus took the stripes for our healing. He was mocked, beaten, and gorged from head to toe for our healing. He hung on a cross and bled from the thorned, fake crown, and everywhere, He had been pierced for us to overcome our trials and tribulations. He died for *us*. But, He rose from the grave to let us know that He lives and because of that, we can face tomorrow and whatever it brings. He wanted to let us know that if He could come back from the grave, nothing was too big, too small, or impossible for Him. We must learn to trust and believe that He is our Savior and wants us to someday be with Him in paradise.

All He wants is for us to give Him our praise and worship. He wants us to open our mouths about His grace and His mercy. I thought that telling my story to others was going to be difficult, because I stopped working the night before my brain surgery. And, since the surgeries, Curtis and my daughters have requested that I don't go back to work. I'll be sixty-five in a few months, and I know that God has given me a second chance at life, and I'm going to use it to the max. I feel like it's time for me to spend more time with my grandchildren. So, I did not think that I would have much of an opportunity to spread the Word, or share my story, since most of my days are with toddlers and they have been my new world. But, somehow, I still have been in a position almost every single day to share my testimony with someone. I find myself at the grocery store, shopping centers, parking lots, and even kids' birthday parties, giving my testimony and trying to lead others to God's kingdom. It sounded like it was going to be an impossible assignment to complete. But, God specializes in *doing* the impossible.

Now that a few months have passed, I am starting to feel like my old self. I have good days and *great* days! Good days are the days that God allows me to wake up. Great days are the days where I feel close to normal, if there is such a thing anymore. I have a tee-shirt that reads, "Normal is not coming back, but Jesus is." I love that shirt and think it is accurate with the way our world seems to be going these days. In my case, I won't complain. In less than five months, I have had six surgeries, a few months of aggressive chemotherapy, and too many tests to even count, with no pain or suffering. The few aches I may have had were all resolved with Tylenol or ice, so I feel blessed. Things could have been much different for me. When I was in the chemo treatment room, there were so many patients, that by looking at them, you knew they had given up and had no hope. Cancer does not have to be a death sentence. I spent time in there praying for others that had given up and reminding them that God is still on the throne. I opened my mouth and let others know that God is still in the miracle-making business.

Don't talk defeat over your situation; practice trying to live in the spirit of expectancy, knowing your victory is coming. The tongue is a powerful tool. It can speak life or death into something. Instead of looking at the glass of water halfway empty, make the choice to see it halfway full. Know that with God, your glass can be *all* the way full. Do not settle for anything less. It does not matter if it is a health issue that you were told was not curable, like with me, or something more serious. It could be that bank loan or credit card you were denied. It could be unseen problems with your spouse or children. Maybe you received a rejection letter from the college of your choice, or a job that you thought you nailed at the interview. Your car may be on its way to being repossessed or you may be losing your home to a foreclosure. Please understand that nothing is too big or too small for God to handle. He not only can do the impossible, but he can do it in a moment's time. I am a witness and the walking truth of how He works. All you must do is trust and believe that He is Lord over everything and everyone.

UPMC, the conglomeration of state-of-the-art medical facilities in our state, reached out to me a few months after my lung surgery. They said that I had been reported by doctors and nurses to their marketing team as someone they should speak with, based on my experience. When they called, I was asked to tell them my story of what I had gone through within the last five months. Afterwards, they told me that my story was one that should be shared with other patients to give them hope. They asked me if I would be interested in writing a testimonial that they could put on their website. I said yes, and they told me they would get back with me. Two days passed, and I received another call from the marketing department. Ashley, the representative, said she heard my story and believed that a video should accompany the testimonial; she asked if I would be interested in letting them shoot a video. I said yes. They told me they would set up an appointment via Zoom, for me to meet with the marketing team and tell my story. I was emailed an appointment time to meet with them and asked to confirm the date and time, which I did. I met with the team, and at the end of the meeting, they told me they loved my story and thought a video of my story would be an inspiration to others who were looking down a dark road. I agreed. The next day, I received a call from Ashley in the marketing department, and she said that after the meeting, they discussed my case and were all in agreement that they should work a full TV commercial around my story. So, they set up a date and time, and a few weeks later, recorded the audio of me for the voice over in the commercial. I reminded them that in my story I told them that God led me to UPMC, and I did not want Him to be left out. They agreed that my faith would not be edited out.

Two weeks later, they filmed the commercial. It was quite the experience. They asked me to invite my husband Curtis, my daughters, their spouses, and my "lady bugs" to be in the commercial. They had me take pictures around my house, and as many pictures of my family pictures as possible. They rented a beautiful house for the filming, and when we walked into the house for the first time, there were pictures of my family framed and sitting everywhere. They even asked me to bring our family Bible that I had sent in, as well as our picture of Christ on the cross. It made us feel like we were at home. They filmed for more than nine hours, all to edit down to sixty seconds. By the end of the day, we were all tired, but it was a lot of fun for the entire family. They told us it would take a few weeks to edit, and about three months before it would air. I was excited because I knew this commercial would honor God. I saw it as an opportunity for me to open my mouth and let others know that He is a miracle worker.

I was feeling great and ready to celebrate what God had brought me through. The lung surgeon asked me not to fly right away, but that he was ok with me taking a vacation that was not too strenuous. Right away, Curtis and I started trying to figure out the right vacation that would not jeopardize my recovery. We decided on a cruise. It seemed perfect. There was a Carnival Cruise port less than two hours from our home, so we could drive there to board. And, as far as the doctor's orders that the vacation could not be too strenuous, nothing is more relaxing than a cruise. So, we quickly booked a cruise to the Bahamas.

We had met a nice couple five years back on a cruise and we hit it off right away. Karela was an older hairstylist like me, who also owned her own salon like I did. They had been asking us for years to meet up with them again, but the timing was never right. Either our schedules did not match the dates of the cruise they were taking, or the Covid pandemic got in the way. I was so excited to call Tom and let him know that we were ready to cruise, and see if they were available. After speaking with him, he told us that they booked their cruises months in advance; they were already planning to go out with their children and grands a few months after the cruise we were sailing to the Bahamas, but wish they had known sooner. I explained we were celebrating and that we were ready to go *now*! After I told him the entire story of what I had been through in the last five months with the brain surgery, spine surgery, and the lung surgery, he could not believe it, and was amazed at how I pulled through. He and Karela are both believers, and he understood why we did not want to wait any longer to cruise. He wished us the best and said they would be in touch in a few months to hear about our Bahamas cruise.

A few days later, Tom called and said how much they enjoyed our company on the last cruise, and because their kids were dragging their feet on the cruise they had already planned, they called the cruise agent and booked the same cruise as us to the Bahamas. He said my story touched him and they wanted to celebrate with us. I was so excited that we were finally going to meet back up with Tom and Karela. From that day on, Tom and I started the countdown. Thirty days to go, twenty-five days to go, and then I received a text from him asking me to please call him. I called, and with excitement in my voice, I said, "Only a few weeks to go," but he did not answer. I called his name a few times and when he did try to talk, he was choked up with tears, and it was difficult for him to talk. I knew something was wrong and told him to take his time, and speak when he was ready. When he did stop crying and was able to talk, he told me that Karela had been having some headaches and spells of confusion for a few weeks. He said she had to be rushed to the hospital, and that after a series of test, she was diagnosed with having a tumor on her brain that needed emergency surgery. He said he had thought about what I had just gone through, and felt like I was someone he wanted to talk to about Karela.

I could not believe that she was dealing with the same thing that I had just gone through! We talked for a few minutes, and then I prayed with him. I reminded them both that there was another report, and that Jesus was still on the throne. A few days later, they operated on Karela's brain to remove the mass. Curtis and I prayed for her and Tom daily, and some days, we sent a prayer through text. The surgery went well, and she was recovering fine. She now had to go through chemotherapy or radiation.

I truly believe that the challenges we go through in life are not always for us, but to help someone *else* down the road who may need to hear your story for inspiration to help them get through their challenges. I honestly didn't think it was by coincidence that our paths crossed five years ago, which started our friendship. I truly believe that God put me in her path and brought us back together a month before our planned cruise, and that her diagnosis, which was only two weeks before we were to head out to the Bahamas together. He put me in her path right at the time she needed to hear about how God worked it out for me, so that she might be inspired, knowing that if God did it for me, He would certainly do it for *her*, a true believer. The same faith that healed me, I believe would heal Karela. It felt good to have been planted by God in her path. Truly, He is worthy to be praised.

I sit here now, completing my story, but not my journey. I know God has kept me here in this thing called life for a real purpose. I always knew that we all had a born, given purpose to try to lead others to God's kingdom, where they would have an opportunity to inherit eternal life. But, I never knew that this story would be part of how I would lead them. As I bring this story to a close, I think back on how many cruise mates

I have shared the story of my journey with. I did not have to push it down their throats, nor talk to dead ears. Katherine and her girls, Gina and her family, as well as the lady who gave up her big, comfortable shell-shaped deck chair, where I started writing this last chapter, were all in agreement that God had favored me. They all were planted in my pathway with listening ears, in awe as to what God had done for me. I stand here now on my cabin balcony, looking at the beautiful blue ocean and blue sky. The sunset is breath-taking, and the warm ocean breeze is indescribable. Only God could paint such a beautiful picture. This cruise celebration of the glory of God was the perfect environment to finish my story.

Celebration Cruise.

No matter what trials or tribulations come before us, I am a witness that the same way Jesus's stone was rolled away after His death, God can roll away *our* stone. He can roll away our stone of doubt, fear, anxiety, worry, etc. All He wants us to do is to put it in His hands, then trust, believe, and have faith that He will work it out. The Bible tells us that faith the size of a mustard seed is all we need. Throughout my life, God has showed up and has turned impossible situations around for me, time after time. If I wasn't chosen, I surely feel honored like someone who has been.

If you look back over your life and you think things over, you too may recall getting over things that were totally impossible or not doable. Maybe the odds were against you, and you ended up on top. You may have been in a situation that seemed as though there was no possible way out, and then out of nowhere, things worked out. Maybe, just maybe, you too, were chosen. If so, you too have an awesome responsibility to open your mouth, so that someone else may believe that there's a way, and gain hope, strength, and faith from your experience. The same way God pulled you through your challenging ordeal, He will do the same for them. We overturn the enemy by the blood of the Lamb, and by the words of our testimony.

I am a walking, talking, breathing miracle that God is *still* the Great Physician, and the only drug you need is a small prescription of faith. He already paid the price for us to be healed from anything and any situation that we find impossible. He will work it out for those who believe in Him as

Lord and Savior. And, when He does work it out for you, all He wants is your praise and worship. So, please don't forget to open your mouth and share the good news of Jesus Christ every chance you get. Remember, our challenges in life may just be the ticket for someone else's life. Remember, God is *still* on the throne.

> "And after you have suffered a little while, the God of all grace, who has called you to His eternal glory in Christ, will himself restore, support, strengthen, and establish you. To Him be the power forever and ever."
>
> — 1 Peter 5:10-11

Truly, I thank God that I feel better than ever and back into the swing of things with my "Lady Bugs", Kya, Kali & Baby Khloe.

Acknowledgements

Truly, I feel blessed that throughout my life, I have been supported with love, inspiration, and prayer. The people God has surrounded me with have always believed in my vision. My story would not have been possible without encouragement from many people.

Most of my accomplishments started initially from the guidance of my mother, Agnes Waters Byrd, who taught me from a young age to acknowledge God in all things and that He would direct my path. She carried me to church when I was only eight-weeks old, and I have been there ever since. It was my father, Samuel Byrd, a hard-working man that supported his family and made sure that we wanted for nothing. He worked hard and believed in strong family values. From ballet lessons to me opening my first beauty salon, he made it happen by working extra shifts to financially support my dreams. They both were excellent parents and role models of how a marriage works. They both taught me that leading by example is the best lesson you can teach your children.

To my husband, best friend, and the love of my life for more than thirty-five years, Curtis Moreese George, I thank you for never giving up on me and always being there to support me through all my deficiencies and craziness. Thank you for your patience as I grew into the woman I am today. Thank you for giving me the most beautiful, smartest, and talented daughters I could have ever imagined. Thank you for sharing your family with me. I will never forget Big Ma, who taught me many things. From the time God allowed our paths to cross, when I was your Sunday School teacher to our first date ending with you asking me if you were invited to go to church with me, I knew God had sent you to me. Together we have grown in our ministry as Deacon and Deaconess in our church and I am so proud that you are a true man of God and I'm Honored to call you, my husband.

To Samara Curtiss George, my first born, you have made me a proud mama. Your creativity has surpassed anything I could have ever imagined. You are one of the most courageous people I have ever known. Your spirit is kind and gentle and your beauty inside and out is second to none. You are an asset to the family business, inspiring our students and making sure that the school is always in compliance. Your support and love for me is deeply felt, but it is your love for God that will continue opening doors for you.

To Aynyess Mauryce George, my baby girl, truly, you got a double dose of me and your dad. Your entrepreneurship spirit is hard to keep up with. I feel honored that you have followed in my footsteps and found a way to purchase our family business. Even though you changed the name to the Barber and Beauty Academy of Pennsylvania, we are so proud that you have allowed our legacy to continue helping and guiding young cosmetologists and barbers. You are an awesome soul mate and mother. You and Kyle McDonald have given me a wonderful gift, my three lady bugs. It's so obvious that God's blessings have been in overflow for you both. Please continue to acknowledge Him and keep Him first in your life and your cup will runneth over.

To my granddaughters, The Lady Bugs, Kya, Kali and Khloe McDonald, you three little bugaboos have been my inspiration for everything. You have expanded my world and have made it clear that you are part of God's purpose for keeping me alive. Even though you are only toddlers, I see a bright future for you all. Remember to honor your mommy and daddy and kept God first in your life. Cocomelon will eventually have an ending season with you, but God never will.

To Greyson Prescott Fields, my grandson, you are the most talented, intelligent, and handsome young man in our family. Continue the road you are on, and it will bring you much success. Remember, it is only by the hand of God that you are so ahead of the game. Remember to always mind your manners and your mom and doors will open that will bring you much happiness.

To Stephanie Byrd Fair and Marsha Blackston, my sisters, who have supported me even when you knew my plan wasn't gonna work. You both have been much more than my big sisters. You both have been examples of great wives, great mothers, and great friends. I love you both, your children, and grandchildren. Thank you for all your inspiration and encouragement throughout the years and for always treating me like Sugie, your baby sister.

To Pastor and First Lady Aigner Dockens and my entire Trinity Church of God family, who supported me through a journey that *only* God could see me through. Your prayers, gifts, food, cash, love, and support were deeply felt and truly helped me.

To all my friends, classmates, family members, churches, neighbors, and strangers who prayed for me, I love you and thank you for being so thoughtful.

> The Word tells us: The effectual fervent prayer of a righteous man availeth much.

> — James 5:16